From Van Valkenburg to Vollick

V. 2: Cornelius Vollick and his Follick and Vollick Descendants to 3 Generations

by Lorine McGinnis Schulze

Cover image 1835 Watercolour by Robert Petley
Credit: Library and Archives Canada, Acc. No. 1938-220-1, C-115424

Cornelius Vollick & Eve Larroway 1

Documents for Cornelius and Eve Vollick 6

Isaac Vollick & Sophia Burkholder 18

Matthias Vollick & Catherine Burkholder 39

Mary Vollick & Albert Bradt 46

Peter Vollick & Nancy Hanart 54

Janine Vollick & Jacob Burkholder 59

Eliza Vollick & Richard Lightheart & Jacob Burkholder 61

Richard Vollick & Elizabeth Burkholder 63

Margaret Vollick & David Burkholder 69

The Larroway Family 71

The Burkholder Family 74

Family Photographs 84

Newspaper Clippings 105

Endnotes 109

Cornelius Vollick & Eve Larroway

Cornelius Vollick was born 16 August 1761 in Albany New York [1] to Isaac Van Valkenburg and Maria Warner. He died after 1818 in Upper Canada (present day Ontario). For the story of his parents and their ancestry, see *"From Van Valkenburg to Vollick: V. 1 The Loyalist Isaac Van Valkenburg aka Vollick and his Vollick & Follick Children"* by Lorine McGinnis Schulze.

Volume 1 is the story of Isaac Vollick, a Loyalist who fought with Butler's Rangers during the American Revolution. He and his wife Anna Maria (Mary) Warner settled in Upper Canada in 1782. Isaac's Land Petitions, Affidavits of witnesses regarding his Loyalty to the British Crown, letters about Mary's ordeal after American Patriots burned her home and sent the family fleeing north to Canada in 1779, and other records are found in Volume 1. Stories of Isaac's ancestors back to the first settlement of New Amsterdam (present day New York City) and Albany in the 1620s and Mary's ancestors back to the 1709 Palatine immigration from Germany to New York are included.

Cornelius Vollick married Eve Larroway on 24 March 1795 in Niagara, Ontario. [2] His wife Eve was born 14 March 1776 in Berne, Albany Co., New York to the Loyalist Jonas Larroway and his wife Elizabeth Muller.

Please note that throughout this book I have used Cornelius and the interchangeable Cornelis since that is how his name appears in various records.

In 1782 Cornelius is listed as living at Niagara Ontario with disbanded Butler's Rangers and their families. His parents and siblings are also living there at that time. Although he is not listed as a soldier on the roster for Butler's Rangers he was able to obtain land as the son of a Loyalist.

17 August 1795 he is in Newark Ontario. Cornelius son of Isaac was recorded as a supporter of the Church at St. Catharines in 1795 [3]

On 10 March 1797 Cornelius received a free grant of 200 acres of land Concession 5, Lot 7 East Flamborough Township Ontario as Cornelius Fallock [sic]

Dickson, William - Stating that he has applied to the secretary of the province accompanied by Mr. Clinch, attorney for Cornelius Folluck, for a deed in said Folluck's name, that from a small difference in the spelling of the father and the son's name, it is still refused, although by an order of Council the secretary is directed to put His Majesty's service and Council to as little delay as possible and praying for the deed in question. Ordered, that the secretary do deliver the deed to the person named in the power of attorney. [4]

24 Oct. 1812: In the 1st. Regiment Lincoln Militia a Cornelius Vollick is listed as age 37 and "ruptu'd". It is possible the age was meant to be 51 and was misread - it is easy to confuse a 3 with a 5 and a 1 with a 7 in old records. We do not know with certainty this is our Cornelius. It could possibly be a son.

1819 Assessment Nelson Township Gore District: Cornelius Follick [sic] is living beside Isaac Bradt and Albert Bradt. Cornelius has 50 uncultivated acres in Gore District, 1 horse, 2 oxen, 1 milk cow, 1 horned cattle. His total aggregate amount is 30 and his assessment is 20 pounds 6 shillings. Note that Albert Bradt married Mary Vollick

1830 census Nelson Township Gore District shows Cornelius Volk living beside Jonas Volk and near Peter Volk.

He is listed as head of a family of 9 consisting of 1 son over 16, 4 sons under 16, and 2 daughters under 16. This is likely Cornelius and Eve - we know that Isaac, Jonas and Mathias are all married, leaving Richard as the possible son over 16 (he would be 21). Of his probable daughters, Margaret is possibly married in 1830, leaving Eliza and Janine as the two daughters under 16. This leaves us with 4 more sons, born between 1814 and 1830.

The only child we have positively confirmed as a child of Cornelius and Eve is Margaret Vollick born 1815. The other children I have assigned to Cornelius and Eve are placed there based on naming patterns, dates of birth in conjunction with parents' marrriage date, land locations, and other circumstantial evidence. It is important to note that early Ontario records are few and far between. Those that do exist are scattered in different repositories, making research challenging.

The Lutheran Church in Thorold was near the crossroads leading from Homer to Thorold and from St. Davids to Thorold and points west. Surnames of some of the subscribers were Aker, Ball, Beamer, Brown, Crysler, Dittrick, **FALK**, Fralick, Grass, Hansel, Hainer, Haines, Hartsell, Honsinger, Hoover, Hutt, Killman, Lampman, **LARROWAY**, May, Metler, Meller, Schram, Smith, Stull, Weaver, and Wright.

In 1802 Jacob BALL Jr. donated 6 acres for the church Manse, schoolhouse and burying ground to the Lutheran and Presbyterian Church. The church was later known as "The Old German Church". Supporters for the German Church ca 1803 were: Jno BROWN, **Cornelius FALK [Vollick]**, Jno HAINER, Wm. MAY, Zachariah HANES, **Benj. CRUMB** [married Cornelius' sister Sarah Vollick], Adam HANES, Jno HONSINGER Sr., Geo. HANSEL, Frederick SCHRAM, Geo. SLOUGH, Adrian BRADT, Benj. FRALICK, Derick HANES [probably Derrick Hayner, husband of Cornelis' sister Annetje Vollick], Jno. FRALICK, Jonas LARAWAY [brother in law or father-in-law of Cornelis], Jeremiah SCHRAM, Albert HAINER [Married to Cornelius' sister], Nicholas SMITH, Christian BRADT, Wm. OSTERHOUT, Henry SMITH, Frederick SMITH, Jacob

DEDERICK, Christopher BEAMER, Wm. MILLER, Jno. HONSINGER Jr., Jno. HARRIS, Isaac FALK [Vollick], Wm. FALK [Vollick]

ANGLICAN CHURCH, ST. CATHARINES (1795 - 1836) On this site stood the Anglican chapel, St. Catharines (1795 - 1836), the first public building in the community. The name St. Catharines became associated with the community and the church. By 1797 a log school house was situated just east of this spot. The Parish included a cemetery and a parsonage. An assignment to the church dated Feb. 17, 1796 is the first documented use of the City's name and records the names of the 44 heads of the community's founding families and others from the surrounding area. John Backhouse, John Hayner, Jacob Dittrick, Abraham Clendenin, Benjamin Froilick, Henry Smith, Zackariah Hayner, Richard Hayner, Albert Hayner, Adam Haynes, **Cornelius Follock**, John Decow, Robert Campbell, John Turney, John Brown, William Day, Obediah Hopkins, Peter Hopkins, Asa Waterhouse, John Willson Senr., Hugh Willson, John Kelly, Jonathan Nunn, George Couke, Jacob Upper, Anthony Upper, Petter Wever, George Hover, Stephen Seburn, Philip Metler, Andrew Hanseler, Jacob Bowman, George Keefer, Michael Teattor, Jacob Ball Jr., George Hartsell, John Stevens, Adam Hunt, John Dennis, John Bessey, James Newkirk, Francis Wever, Robert Bessey, Jabish Bessey [This plaque was erected by the St. Catharines Bicentennial Committee with the assistance of the Ontario Heritage Foundation, July 1, 1996]

Children of Cornelius Vollick and Eve Larroway were:
+   2   i.   **Isaac[9] Vollick** was born 24 Apr 1796 in Nelson Township Halton Co. Ontario. [5] , and died 30 Apr 1864 in Nelson Township Halton Co. Ontario [6] He married **Sophia Burkholder** About 1827, daughter of David Burkholder and Elizabeth Gingerich. She was born About 1810 in Hamilton, Barton Township Wentworth Co. Ontario, and died Bet. 1881 - 1891 in Kilbride, Nelson Township Halton Co. Ontario [7]

+   3   ii.   **Jonas Vollick** was born Jul 1797 in Upper Canada, and died 05 Jan 1877 in East Flamborough Township Halton Co. Ontario. [8] He married **Mary Gilbert** Before 1825 in Ontario. She was born About 1805, and died 08 Jun 1865 in Kilbride, Halton Co. Ontario.

+   4   iii.   **Matthias Follick** was born Bet. 1798 - 1800 in St. Catharines Ontario, and died 11 Jan 1870 in Hay Township, Huron Co. Ontario. [9] He married **Catharine Burkholder** Before 1826, daughter of David Burkholder and Elizabeth Gingerich. She was born 23 Mar 1812 in Hamilton, Barton Township Wentworth Co. Ontario, and died 18 Jan 1864 in Hay Township, Huron Co. Ontario. [10]

+   5   iv.   **Mary Vollick** was born 01 Aug 1801 in Louth Township Ontario [11], and died 13 Dec 1856 in Nelson Township Halton Co. Ontario. She married **Albert Bradt** About 1825, son of Adrian Bradt and Sophia Vollick. He was born 17 Apr 1791 in Niagara Ontario or New York, and died 15 Apr 1878 in Nelson Township Halton Co. Ontario. [12]

+   6   v.   **Peter Vollick** was born About 1804 in Ontario, and died Aft. 1845. He married **Nancy Hanart** Before 1830. She was born Before 1810 in Port Credit, Ontario, and died Aft. 1845.

+   7   vi.   **Janine Vollick** was born Aft. 1806 in Ontario, and died Before 1848 in Nelson Township Halton Co. Ontario. She married **Jacob Burkholder** Before 1830, son of David Burkholder and Elizabeth Gingerich. He was born 1806 in Ontario, and died 1894 in Maladide Township Elgin Co. Ontario.

+   8   vii.   **Richard Vollick** was born Oct 1809 in Upper Canada, and died 17 Jul 1891 in Hay Township, Huron Co. Ontario. [13]He married **Elizabeth Burkholder** Before 1832 in Ontario, daughter of David Burkholder and Elizabeth Gingerich. She was born About 1816 in Hamilton, Barton Township, Wentworth Co. Ontario, and died Bet. 1871 - 1881 in Hay Township, Huron Co., Ontario [14]

+   9   viii.   **Margaret Vollick** was born 14 May 1815 in Upper Canada, [15] and died Before 12 Jan 1852 in Middleton Township Norfolk Co. Ontario. [16] She married **David Burkholder** 1831, son of David Burkholder and Elizabeth Gingerich. He was born 1808 in Ontario, and is thought to have died 09 Jun 1882 in Middleton Township, Norfolk Co.

+   10 ix.   **Eliza Follick** was born About 16 May 1817 in Ontario, and died 05 Jun 1892 in Malahide, Elgin Co. Ontario. [17] She married **(1) Richard Lightheart** 04 Mar 1844 in Nelson Township Halton Co. Ontario. [18] He died Before 1848. She married **(2) Jacob Burkholder** 09 May 1848, son of David Burkholder and Elizabeth Gingerich. He was born 1806 in Ontario, and died 1894 in Jarvis, Maladide Township Elgin Co. Ontario. He is buried in Luton Cemetery in Malahide with his wife Eliza. Her name on the tombstone is Elizabeth it reads 1818-1893. Jacob was the widower of Janine Vollick, sister to Eliza

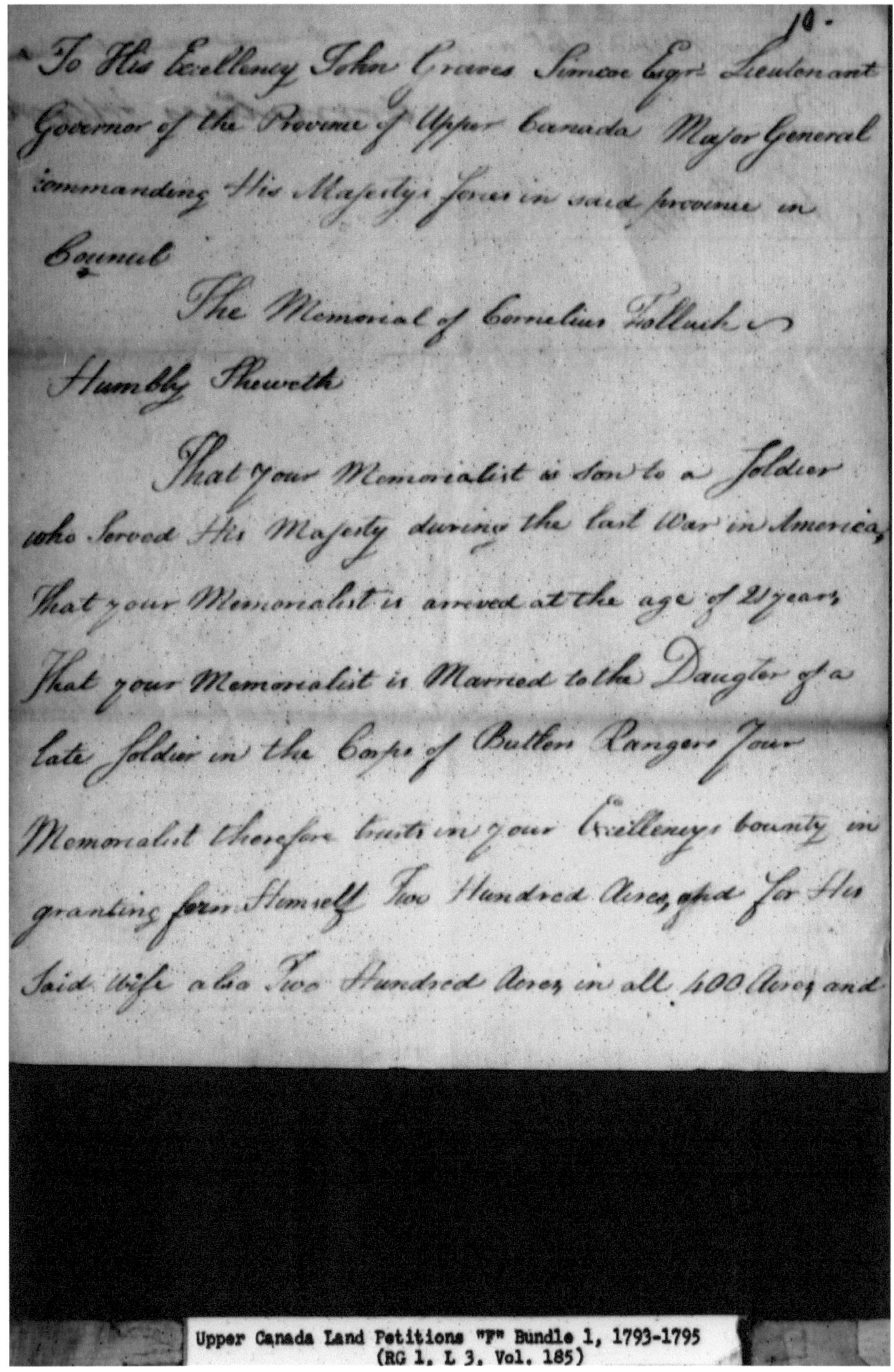

To His Excellency John Graves Simcoe Esqr Lieutenant
Governor of the Province of Upper Canada Major General
commanding His Majesty's forces in said Province in
Council

    The Memorial of Cornelius Folluck

Humbly Sheweth

    That your Memorialist is Son to a Soldier
who Served His Majesty during the last War in America,
That your Memorialist is arrived at the age of 21 years,
That your Memorialist is Married to the Daughter of a
late Soldier in the Corps of Butlers Rangers Your
Memorialist therefore trusts in your Excellencys bounty in
granting for Himself Two Hundred Acres, and for His
Said Wife also Two Hundred Acres, in all 400 Acres and

20 July 1795. Petition for land submitted by Cornelius Folluck. States he is the son of a soldier who served His Majesty during the late war in America. He has reached 21 years of age (this does not mean he is 21, just that he is 21 or over), is married to the daughter of a late soldier in the Corps of Butler's Rangers and wishes 200 acres in his wife's name and another 200 for a total of 400 acres. Ends with his signature Cornelius Follock.

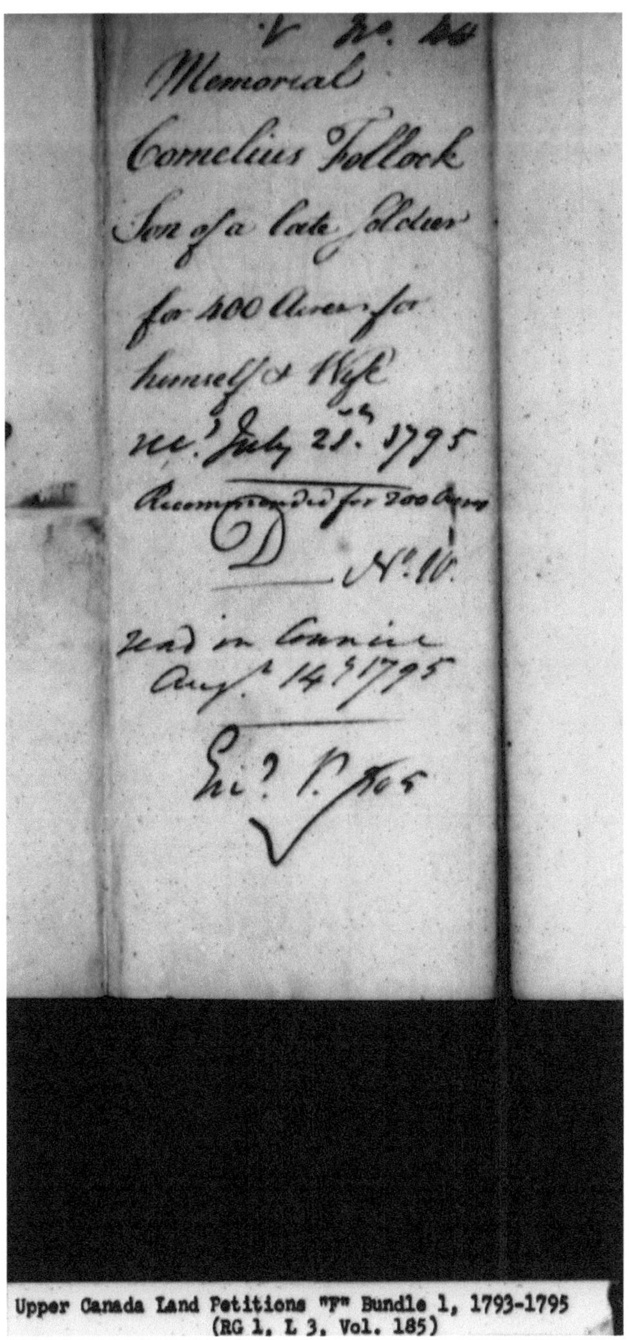

The envelope provides the result of his plea for land. He was recommended for 200 acres, not 400.

Weddings   Niagara 1795

January

20   John Carr Bachelor and Ann FitzGerald Widow

March

3   John Chrysler and Elizabeth Morden Spin[r]

9   Mathew Wormwood and Margaret Wintermute

15   William Wallace Bach[r] and Ann Douale Spin[r]

24   Cornelius Volick B[r] and Eve Lorraway Spin[r]

April   <---Cornelius & Eve

11   James McBride Bach[r] & Sarah Read Widow

13   Peter Whitney B[r] & Margaret Baynes Spinster

May

3   Israel Birch B[r] & Deborah Bellinger [Wid]

19   James Muirhead Bach[r] & Deborah Butler Spin[r]

June

[...] Johnston Spin[r]

Marriage of Cornelius Vollick & Eve Larroway. April 1795

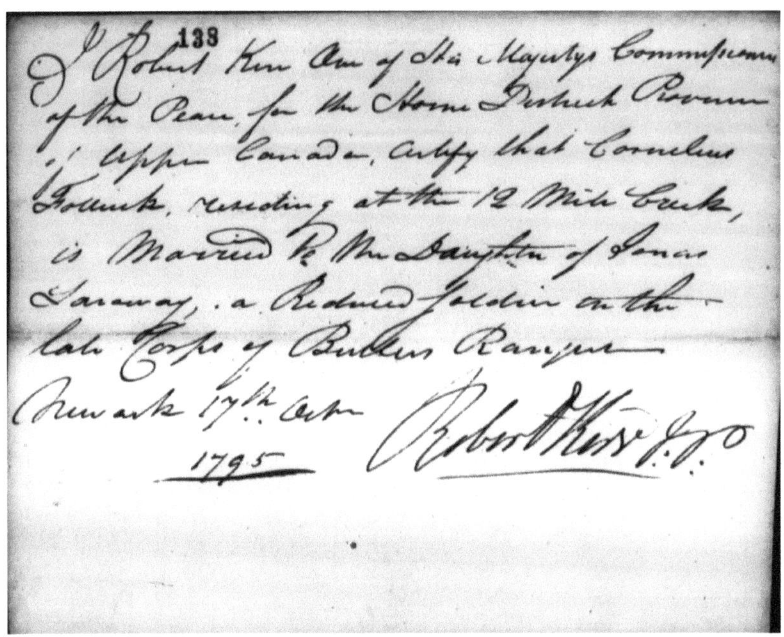

Heir & Devisee Commission H-1146 Page 138

Newark 17 October 1795. Robert Kerr certifies that Cornelius Folluck (sic), residing at 18 Mile Creek, is married to the daughter of Jonas Laraway, a reduced soldier in the late Corps of Butler's Rangers

Envelope for Cornelius Follock (sic) p. 139

Newark, 3 March1796. Petition submitted by Cornelius Follock. He states he is the son of Isaac Follock who served his Majesty during the late war in Col. Butler's Corps of Rangers. He has drawn 200 acres of land in his own right, but being married to the daughter of Jonas Laraway, an old soldier and U.E. wishes 200 acres in his wife's right.

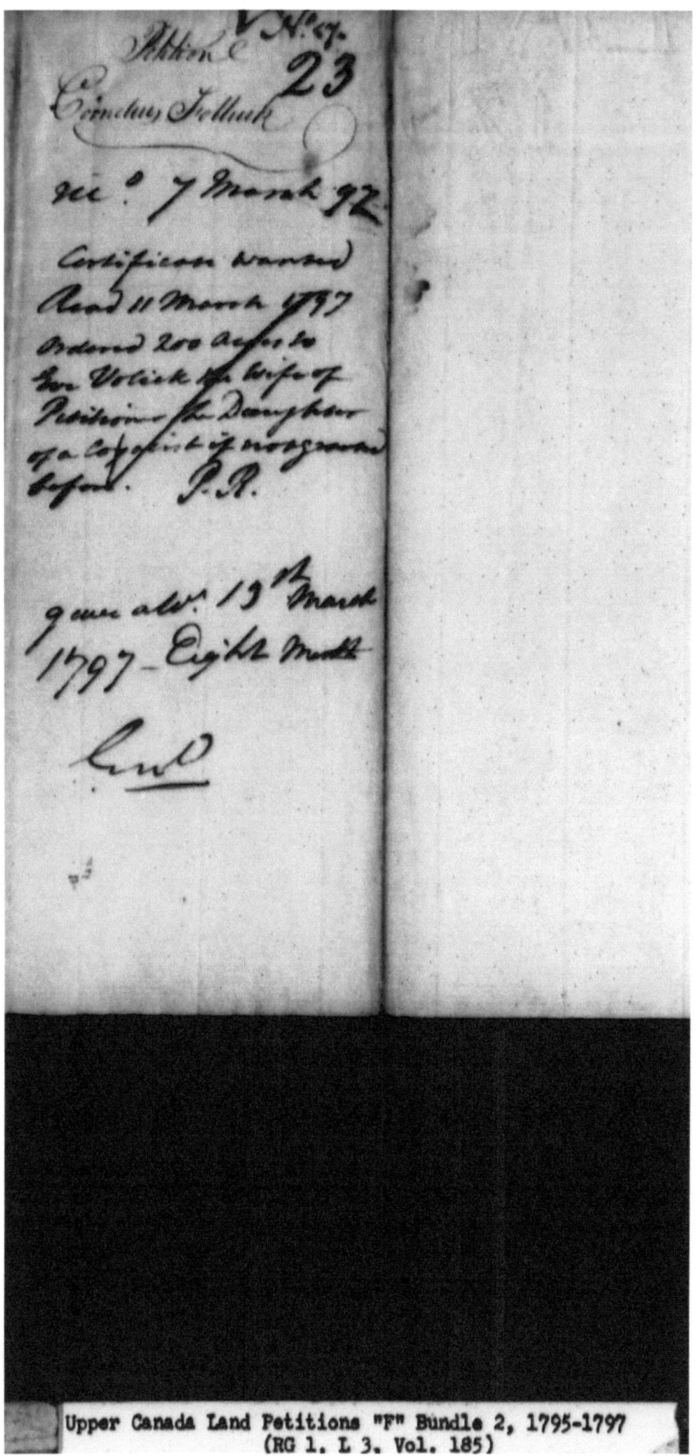

Envelope shows the final decision. 200 acres is granted to Eve Vollick on 7 March 1797.

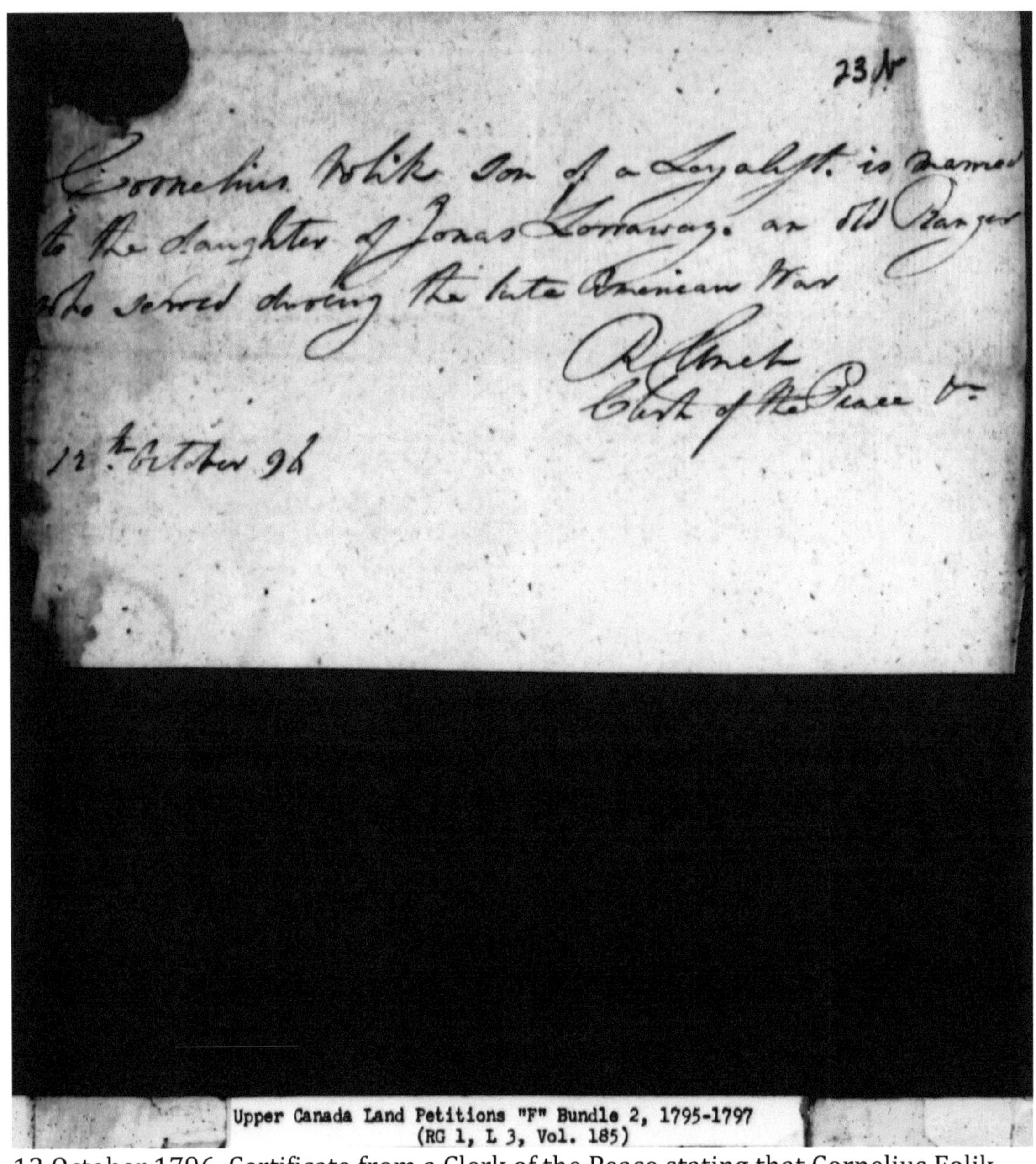

Upper Canada Land Petitions "F" Bundle 2, 1795-1797
(RG 1, L 3, Vol. 185)

12 October 1796. Certificate from a Clerk of the Peace stating that Cornelius Folik (sic) son of a Loyalist, is married to the daughter of Jonas Laraway, an old Ranger who served during the late American War

Queenston 12 April 1799. Bond to Robert Hamilton of Queenston from Isaac Volluck and Cornelius Volluck, both of Home District of Upper Canada, yeoman. They are bonded for 100 pounds of lawful money. Whereas Cornelius Volluck is to receive 200 acres of land on account of his wife, the daughter of a Loyalist, he has consented to sell the land for 20 pounds to Robert Hamilton

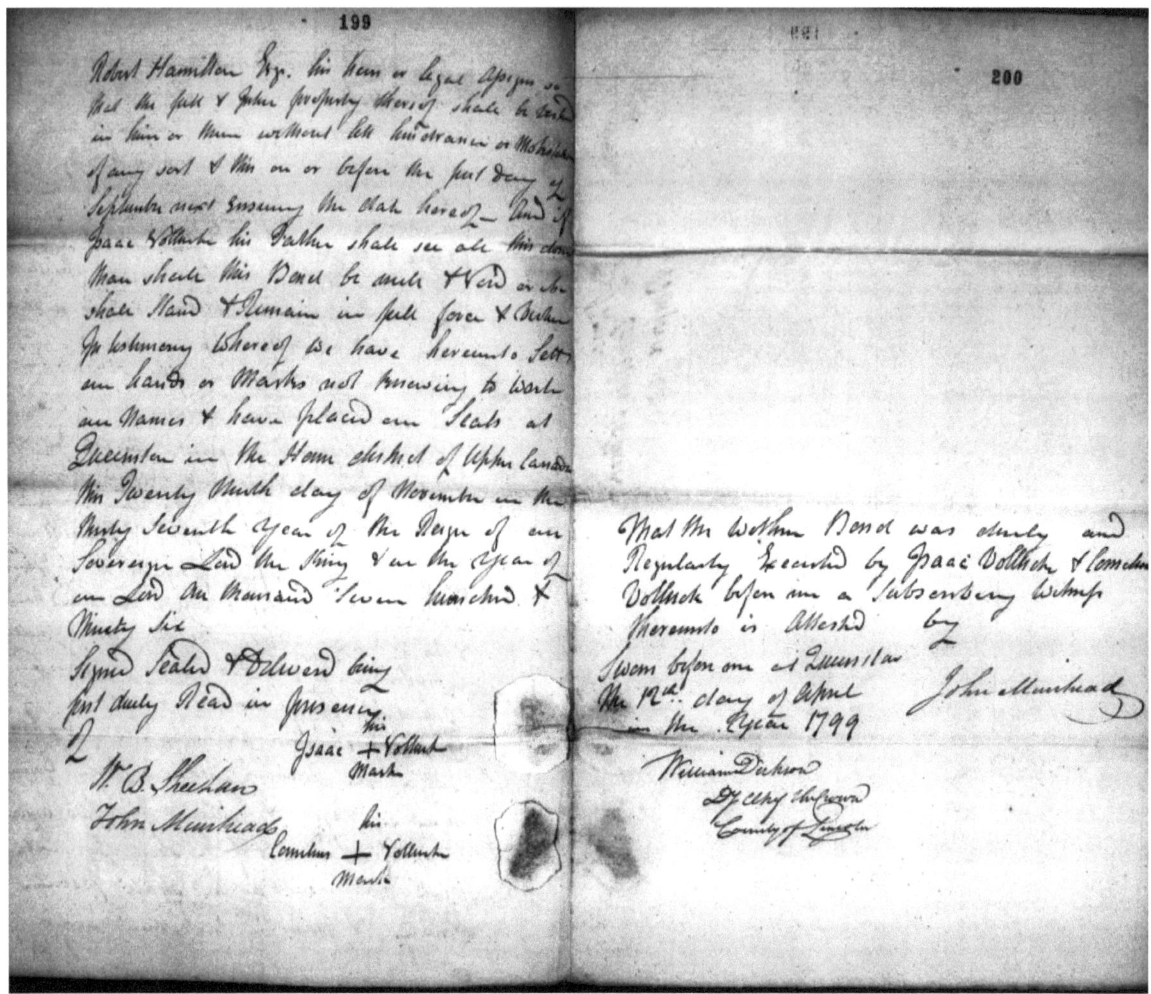

Isaac is mentioned as being the father of Cornelius. They both make their marks.

Burford

153

Names	Lot	Con	Acres	
[illegible name]	7	13	200	in his Bond
Christian Bratt	12	9	200	in his Bond
Joseph Biggar	14	10	200	Do
Roger Blan	23	10	200	Do
Asa Dayton	2	10	200	Do
John Good	22	9	200	Do
John Hart	10	9	200	Do
Rich.d Hainer	N½ 12	10	150	Do
Dorothy Hainer	24	11	250	in Bond of Albert Hainer
Jonas Larroway	11 & N½ 12	10	250	in his Bond
Geo. Shusman	16 / ½ 15	10 / 11	300	Do
Cornelius Vollick	21	2	200	in Do in his wife
Marg.t Whitney	21	10	200	in Bond P. Whitney
Philip Young	22	11	200	in Bond

carried forward 2850

Heir & Devisee Commission Film H-1144. Supporting documents for claims in Burford Township 1796-1799. Cornelius Vollick is listed as receiving 200 acres (Concession 2, Lot 21) in his wife's right. I suspect this is the land he sold to Robert Hamilton. Notice also his relatives: Jonas Larroway 250 acres Concession 10, Lot 12 (probably his wife Eve's brother); Dorothy Hainer 250 acres on Concession 11, Lot 24 in right of her father Albert Hainer who was married to Cornelius' sister Catherine; Christian Bratt (sic) who was married to Cornelius' sister Elizabeth, 200 acres Concession 9, Lot 12; Richard Hainer who was married to Cornelius' sister Annejte 250 acres on Concession 10, Lot 12. All these invididuals gave their bond which no doubt indicates they sold their land in Burford.

Assessment Roll for the Township of Nelson in the District of Gore for the Year 1819

Names	Uncultivated (Gore)	Arable Pasture & Meadow (Gore)	Uncultivated (London)	Cultivated (London)	Uncultivated (Home District)	Cultivated (Home District)	Square under two Stories	Framed under two Stories	Framed two Stories	Additional fire places	wrought by water with ... pair of stones	additional ... or stones	Saw Mills	Merchant Shops	Store Houses	Stone Houses 3 years & upwards	Horses 3 years & upwards	Oxen four years old & upwards	Milch Cows	Horned Cattle from 2 to 4 years	Aggregate Amount	Rate 8d on Pounds	Assessment
Thomas Atkinson	124	56	100					1									2	2	3	2	170–16–		14 3
James Kitchen																		2	2		16–0–		1 4
George Will																			2	2	24–0–		2
Stephen Barbery	120	30																			85–0–		7 1
Charles Stuart	70	30																	3		61–0–		5 1
John McCollum	200	60															3	2	4		144–0–		12
Philip Snider	100																		1		23–0–		7 11
Isaac Carl			84	40													2		5		87–16–		4
William Lane	16	4															1		1		13–4–		
[blot] Persons	260	40	200					1									2	2	3		184–0–		15 14
Josiah Griffan	170	30			60		1										2	2	5		135–0–		3
Henry Williman	160	20															1		2		58–0–		10
Daniel Will	70	30															1	2	2		66–0–		5 6
John Shepman	182	18																	4		66–8–		5 6
Moses McCoy	60	40			280												2	2	4	2	90–0–		
Abraham O'Strander	10	10																	1		15–0–		
Cornelius Vollick	50																1	2	1		30–0–		1 6
Isaac Bradt	50																1		1		18–0–		1 6
Albert Bradt	50																1		1		21–0–		1 9

1819 Assessment Nelson Township, Gore District. Cornelius Vollick is 3rd name from bottom.

Isaac Vollick & Sophia Burkholder

Isaac & Sophia lived under Bradt's Peak, Lowville, Ontario.

Isaac Vollock [sic] age 34 is listed in 2nd. Regiment Gore Militia, Nelson Township as of 22 Dec. 1828 [#92] This could be the same Isaac VOLLOCK who is on the Muster Roll & Paylist of Cptn. George Law's Co. 1st. Reg. Lincoln Militia 19-24 Sept. 1813. He served 6 days for 3 shillings.

The 1832 census for Nelson Township Gore District shows Isaac FOLLICK living on the East side of the east corner of Lot 4 conc 4 with 4 cultivated and 1 uncultivated acre. He is a single male over the age of 16.

The 1842 census Nelson Township Gore District lists Isaac VOLICK [sic] as a labourer on land owned by Thomas Alton. He is the head of a family of 6, all natives of Canada. He has one male under 5 [Joseph?]; one female under 5 [Harriet?], 1 male aged 5 to 14 [Richard?] and one female aged 5 to 14 [?]. He is listed as married aged 30 to 60; his wife as married age 14 to 45. He has cultivated 60 bushels barley, 12 bushels peas, 100 bushels potatoes, and owns 7 cattle, 6 horses and 4 sheep.

1851 Census Nelson Tp Halton Co, Part 2

36	Isaac Follick	Labourer	—	"		X	56
37	Sophia "	Housekeeper		"		X	42
38	Richard "	lab		"			16
39	Harriot "	"		"			14
40	Joseph "	"		"			12
41	Mary Jane "		"				9
42	Elizabeth "		"		"		7
43	Nelson "		"		"		4

1861 Nelson Township, Halton Co. [census Dist.5, p.11] Harriet & Jos. listed absent

46	Isaac Vollick	Labourer	U. C	N. C m.	✓	65	1		m
47	Sophia Vollick		U. C	"	✓	50		1	m
48	Richard Vollick	Labourer	U. C	"	✓	24	1		s
49	Mary Jane Vollick		U. C	"	✓	17		1	s
50	Elizabeth Villick		U. C	"	✓	15		1	s

1864 Conc. 5, Lot 1, Nelson Township, Halton Co.

<u>Obituary</u> Hamilton Evening Times article on Isaac Vollick on p 3 on Saturday, May 7, 1864 copied by the paper from the "Champion": *SUDDEN DEATH. We learn that a man by the name of Isaac Vallick, residing on the 5th line Nelson, died suddenly in a fit on Saturday last. Mr. Vallick it appears, has been slightly subject to fits for a length of time, and more especially if he was in trouble. This fit, which proved fatal, was*

supposed to be induced in consequence of his having but the day previous been deprived of a daughter by that stern and relentless messenger - Death. He leaves a family to mourn his demise. Milton Champion

<u>Canadian Champion (Milton) 25 Mar 1869</u>
Nelson Township Co Minutes
Re Mrs. Sophia Vollick closing road allowance situated between Lot 1 4 Conc NS and Lot 11 2nd Con NDS. The road not now used for public travel and wants to erect a house thereon for her own use, provided sufficient roadway be left unoccupied to allow passage of terms when necessay, Carried.

1871 census Nelson, Halton Co

Vollick	Sophia	F	60	—	O
"	Harriet. M	F	32	—	"
"	Mary J	F	27	—	"
"	Elizabeth	F	25	—	"
"	Nelson	M	22	—	"
"	Charles	M	18	—	"
"	Cyrus	M	12	—	"

1881 Census Place: Nelson, Halton, Ontario, Canada

Vollick Sophiah	F	76	"	"	Germany	—	w
" Harriet	F	42	"	"	"	—	
" Mary L	F	37	"	"	"	Tailoress	—
" Elizabeth	F	35	"	"	"	—	m
" Cirus	m	22	"	"	"	Farm Lab.	

Isaac Vollick and Sophia Burkholder were married about 1827. They had the following children:

i. John Vollick was born after 1827.

ii. William Vollick was born about 1827 in Upper Canada. He married Eliza C. Sheller on 02 May 1848 in Nelson Township Halton Co. Ontario. He died after 1861.

iii. Cornelius Vollick was born about 1830.

iv. James Vollick was born between 1832-1834. He died on 20 Sep 1897 in Haldimand Co. Ontario.

v. Richard Wesley Vollick was born on 01 Jan 1837 in Upper Canada. He married Agnes Wray on 26 Dec 1870 in Waterdown, Flamborough Township Ontario. He died on 07 May 1900 in Nelson Township Halton Co. Ontario.

vi. Harriet Matilda Vollick was born in Sep 1838 in Upper Canada. She died on 18 Oct 1914 in Hamilton, Barton Township Wentworth Co. Ontario.

vii. Eliza Vollick was born about 1839 in Ontario.

viii. Joseph Wesley Vollick was born in Dec 1841 in Upper Canada. He married Margaret Lemon on 05 Nov 1862 in Nelson Township Halton Co. Ontario. He died on 08 Apr 1904 in Hamilton, Barton Township Wentworth Co. Ontario.

ix. Mary Jane Vollick was born about 1844. She died on 29 Mar 1890 in Nelson Tp Halton Co. Ontario.

x. Elizabeth Vollick was born in Nov 1845. She died on 03 Apr 1902 in Nelson Tp, Halton Co. Ontario.

xi. William Nelson (Nelson) Vollick was born on 18 Sep 1849 in Nelson Township Halton Co. Ontario. He died on 20 Mar 1929 in Otterville, Barton Township Wentworth Co. Ontario.

xii. Charles Wellington Vollick was born in 1852 in Seaforth. He married Calista Alberta Smith on 24 May 1881 in North Dorchester Township, Middlesex Co. Ontario. He died on 24 Dec 1915 in London Ontario.

Jonas Vollick & Mary Gilbert

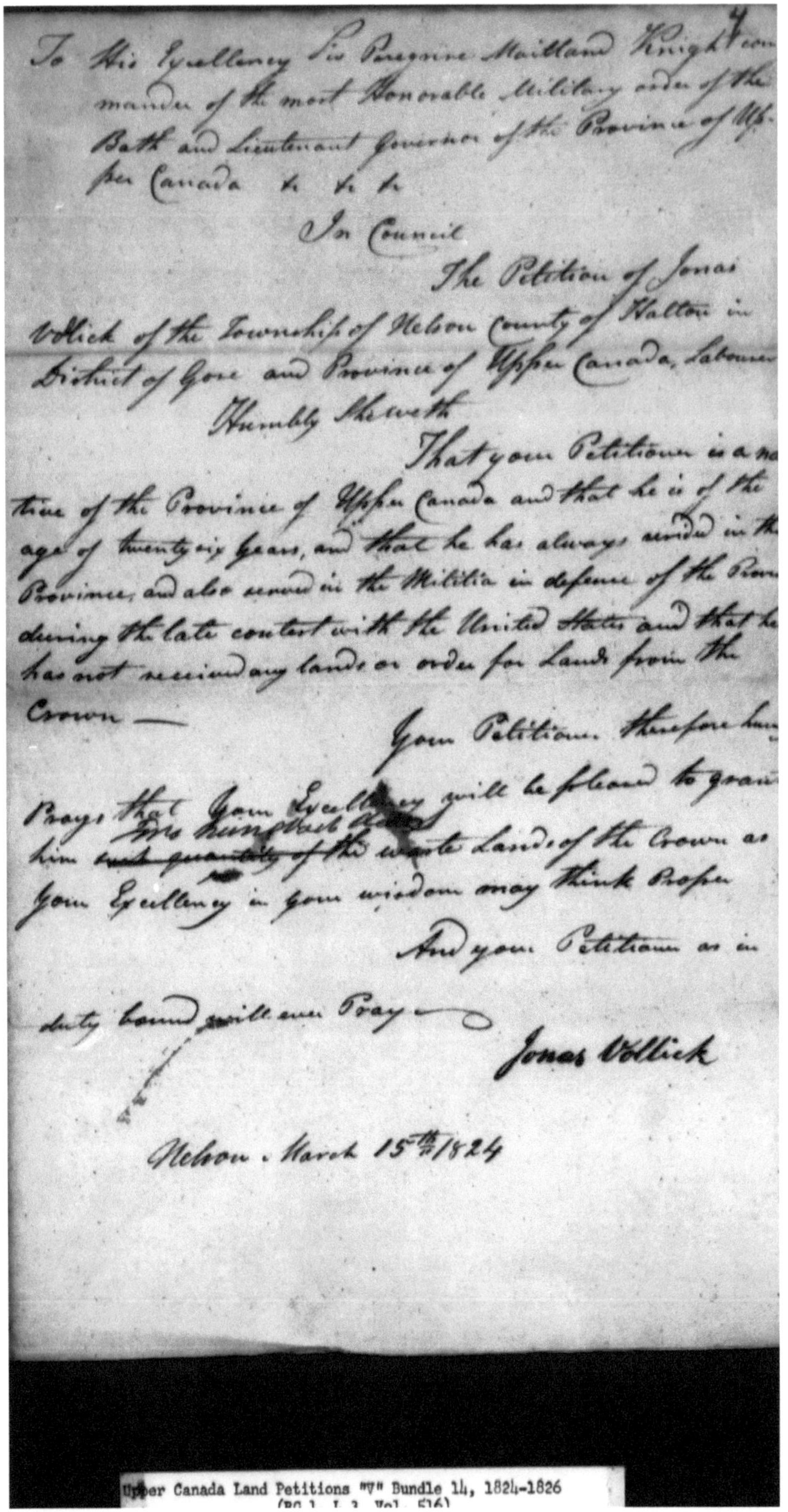

Nelson. 15 March 1824. The petitioner Jonas Vollick of Nelson Township, Halton
County is a native of the country and is of the age of 26 years. States he served in the

militia in the "late conflict" with the United States (War of 1812). He has never received any lands and wishes to be granted 200 acres of Crown Land.

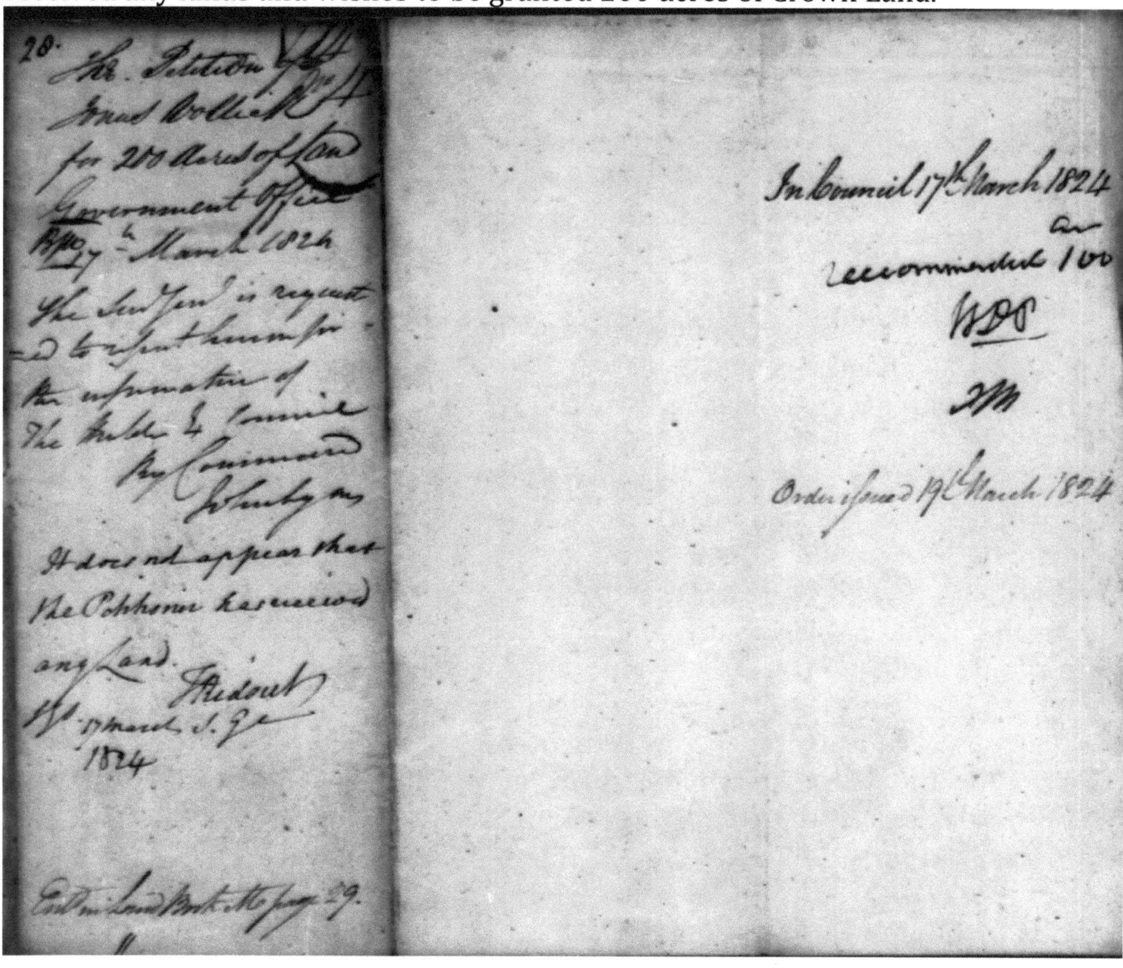

Township Papers, Nelson, MS 658 Reel# 334
Page 234
District of York
Personally came before me Hugh Willson Esquire one of his Majesties Justices of the Peace in and for said District Peter Follick and Jonas Follick both of the Nelson in said district yeoman. Who being duly sworn deposeth and saith that the streets front and near of Lot Number one in the fourth Concessioin of Nelson, New Survey is cleared out two rods wide the whole width of said lot, and that there is ten acres well choped out for growing wheat withn fence, and a House sixteen by twenty feet in the clear built and said lot. Sworn and subscribed before me this second day of June 1824.

Peter X Follick
Jonas X Follick
Hugh Willson J.P.

—

J. Baley

Pte. Richard VOLICK, Age 19 yrs., Line #122, 2nd Regt. GoreMilitia.
Pte. Jas. VOLICK, Age 26 yrs., Line #123, 2nd Regt. Gore Militia.
Pte. John VOLICK, Age 22 yrs., Line #124, 2ndRegt. Gore Militia.
LIMITS: Trafalgar, Nelson & the two Flamboroughs. DATED: 22nd Dec'r. 1828.

1830 census Nelson Township Gore District:

Jonas VOLK [sic] living beside Cornelius VOLK, near Peter VOLK, Jacob PEER and
David BURKHOLDER Sr.

Jonas is head of a family of 4, with one son under 16 and one daughter under 16. If
the order of his children named in his will is the same as their order of birth, then
these two children were William Wesley and Sophia.

1840 census Flamborough East, Microfilm M-7752 District 1 p. 3
Jonas Volic [sic] with 4 males under 16; 2 males over 16; 3 females under 16 and 1
over 16.

His brother Richard Vollick is found on Conc 8 Lot 1 100 acres, East Flamborough
beside Jonas on Conc 7 Lot 1.

1842 census East Flamborough Township Gore District - [MS 700-1 #7-1]:
Jonas Vollick, proprietor, farmer, head of a family of 10, all natives of Canada, and all
Wesleyan Methodists. These numbers fit with his 8 children born before 1842. One
more was born circa 1843-1844.

Jonas has 190 acres, 20 acres improved, 30 bushels wheat, 14 bushels peas, 35
bushels barley, 100 bushels potatoes, 75 lb. maple sugar, 10 neat cattle, 13 sheep, 6
hogs, 7 yds. fulled cloth, 30 yds. flannel home made, and 40 lb. wool.

The 1851 personal census for Flamborough East is missing but we find Jonas in the
1851 Agricultural census for Flamborough East. He is number 8 in the list below.

AGRICULTURAL CENSUS—ENUMERATION DISTRICT, No. 1. in the Township OF

East Flamboro in the **COUNTY OF** Wentworth.

Name of occupier.	Concession or Range.	Lot or part of Lot.	Held by each person or family.	Under Cultivation.	Under Crops in 1851.	Under Pasture 1851.	Gardens or Orchards.	Under Wood or Wild.	Wheat. Acres.	Wheat. Produce Bsh.	Barley. Acres.	Barley. Produce Bsh.	Rye. Acres.	Rye. Produce Bsh.
1	2	3	4	5	6	7	8	9	10	11	12	13	14	15
Allan Miller	6	6	100	30	13	7	0	80	6	60	1½	25	0	0
Geo Ball	6	3	50	30	1½	18½	0	20	3	60	0	0	0	0
Hamilton Kerr	7	3	100	65	17½	46½	1	35	12	230	0	0	0	0
Donald Stewart	6		100	45	30	34	1	55	12	150	24	20	0	0
Edward Blaydes	7	4	100	60	25	35	0	40	10	200	0	0	0	0
Walter Bates	6	1	50	30	10	20	0	20	0	0	0	0	0	0
Bryan Fay	7	2	50	40	24	14½	1½	10	11	100	0	0	0	0
Thos Zillich	7	1	100	70	47	22	1	30	18	350	0	0	0	0

Peas. A	Peas. Bsh.	Oats. A	Oats. Bsh.	B. Wheat. A	B. Wheat. Bsh.	Indian Corn. A	Indian Corn. Bsh.	Potatoes. A	Potatoes. Bsh.	Turnips. A	Turnips. Bsh.	Clover, Timothy or other grass seed—Bsh.	Carrots—Bsh.	Mangle Wurtzel.
16	17	18	19	20	21	22	23	24	25	26	27	28	29	30
1	12	0	0	0	0	0	0	½	50	0	0	0	0	0
1	10	2	40	0	0	0	0	¼	25		30	0	10	0
½	15	½	10	0	0	0	0	1	55	0	20	0	0	0
1	20	1	25	0	0	0	0	½	30	0	0	0	0	0
3	56	1	30	0	0	0	0	1	70	1	300	0	0	0
0	0	0	0	2	20	0	0	1½	100	0	0	0	0	0
2	28	3½	56	0	0	0	0	1¼	250	0	0	0	0	0
6	75	6	120	0	0	1	35	½	75	0	0	0	0	0
3	38	0	0	0	0	0	0	1	50		35	0	0	0

	Beans. Bsh.	Hops. Lbs.	Hay. Bundles or Tons	Flax or Hemp. Lbs.	Tobacco. Lbs.	Wool. Lbs.				Maple Sugar. Lbs.	Cider. Galls.	Fulled Cloth. Yards.	Linen—Yds.	Flannel—Yds.
	31	32	33	34	35	36	37	38	39	40	41	42	43	44
1	0	0	7	0	0	0				100	0	0	0	0
2	0	0	8	0	0	0				10	0	0	0	0
3	0	0	8	0	0	0				0	0	0	0	0
4	0	0	4	0	0	35				0	0	0	0	0
5	0	0	13	0	0	30				0	6	0	0	30
6	0	0	9	0	0	0				0	6	0	0	30
7	0	0	9	0	0	32				0	0	1	0	50
8	0	1	20	0	0	60				0	0	0	0	65
9	0	0	10	0	0	1				0	0	0	0	0
10	0	0	30	0	0	80				0	0	0	0	2 2

	Bulls, Oxen or Steers.	Milch Cows.	Calves or Heifers.	Horses of all ages.	Sheep.	Pigs.	Butter—Lbs.	Cheese—Lbs.	Beef—Barrels or Cwts.	Pork—Barrels or Cwts.	Quantity of Fish Cured.	Remarks.
	45	46	47	48	49	50	51	52	53	54	55	56
1	2	3	0	0	0	3	360	0	0	740	0	
2	4	2	3	0	0	4	150	0	1	600	0	
3	4	3	4	0	0	3	280	0	0	1000	0	The tract of Land
4	2	9	5	4	11	6	760	0	0	450	0	Embraced by this sheet
5	4	2	5	0	0	6	190	0	0	1000	0	well watered, chiefly
6	3	4	3	0	0	5	340	0	500	750	0	by springs.
7	3	30	0	1	4	4	320	0	0	300	0	The Soil is good being
8	1	4	3	2	18	6	700	0	300	1300	0	principally a strong loam
9	3	2	3	0	6	3	160	0	0	760	0	Balance of the Land
10	8	6	5	2	30	8	780	100	0	3000	0	with improvements is
11	2	5	4	2	4	8	720	0	0	800	0	estimated at an average
12	2	2	0	5	0	4	90	0	0	500	0	of about £4 per acre

Jonas Volick, Con 7, Lot 1 with 100 acres; 70 acres are cultivated; 47 acres with crops, 22 acres of pasture, 1 acre garden or orchard and 30 acres woods. His crops were 18 acres of wheat producing 350 bushels; 3 acres of peas producing 38 bushels; 1 acre of potatoes producing 50 bushels; 35 bushels of turnips 20 bundles of hay, 60 lbs of woll, 65 yards of flannel, 1 bull or oxen, 4 milch [milk] cows, 3 calves, 2 horses, 18 sheep, 6 pigs; 700 lbs butter, 300 barrels of beef, 1300 barrels of pork. The census takers notes for this area state "this land is well watered by springs and is good soil"

"From Pathway to Skyway" by Claire Emery and Barbara Ford. Published by Confederation Centennia Commitee of Burlington. Burlington Ontario 1967
Chapter 13: KILBRIDE

In 1853 land on the south side of No. 5 Sideroad west of Cedar Springs Road had been deeded by John Prudham to the trustees. Mr. Prudham's homestead south of Kilbride had been a stopping place for itinerant ministers. Mr. Prudham and Mathias Canon both of Nelson, along with Jonas Vollick, Andrew Davidson and Richard Vollick were the original trustees of the small church of the Methodist New Connexion called Bethel Chapel. The union of exiting Methodist bodies caused Bethel to close about 1874 but a committee of trustees was appointed to care for the grounds and cemetery.

1861 Census East Flamborough D-4 p. 58 Line 39

#	Name		Birthplace	Religion		Age			
32	Jonas Vollick	H	6 W O	N C M	✓	63	1		M
33	Mary Do		Do	Do	✓	57		1	M
34	Joseph Do	1	Do	W M	✓	24	1		M
35	Sarah A Do		Do.	Do	✓	21	1		M
36	Morris H Do		Do	Do	✓	2	1		S

1861 Agricultural Census E. Flamboro shows Jonas Vollick on Line 6:

AGRICULTURAL CENSUS, Enumeration District No. Four of the Township of East Flamboro

Name of Occupier (1)	Concession or Range (2)	Lot or part of Lot (3)	Total held by each Person or Family (4)	Under Cultivation (5)	Under Crop in 1860 (6)	Under Pasture in 1860 (7)	Under Orchards or Garden (8)	Under Wood or Wild (9)	Cash value of Farm, Dollars (10)	Cash value of Farming Implements or Machinery, Dollars (11)	Fall Wheat Acres (12)	Fall Wheat Produce in Bushels (13)	Spring Wheat Acres (14)	Spring Wheat Produce in Bushels (15)	Barley Acres (16)	Barley Produce in Bushels (17)	Rye Acres (18)	Rye Produce in Bushels (19)
Charles Newell	7	182	200	150	60½	8½	3½	50	7000	536	30	910	3½	100	7	230		
John Mullin	7	2	50	44	19	25		6	1200	8	10	100	1	60				
John Kerr	7	3	50	40	12¼	27¾		10	1200	30	6½	100			4	20		
Alexander Kerr	7	5	100					100	600									
Edward Blagden	7	37·4	150	110	59½	50½		40	5000	500	30	590	5	125	9	250		
Jonas Vollick	7	1	99	72	34½	35½	2	27	4000	35	19	436	7	90				

County of Wentworth   74

Peas Acres (20)	Peas Produce in Bushels (21)	Oats Acres (22)	Oats Produce in Bushels (23)	Buck Wheat Acres (24)	Buck Wheat Produce in Bushels (25)	Indian Corn Acres (26)	Indian Corn Produce in Bushels (27)	Potatoes Acres (28)	Potatoes Produce in Bushels (29)	Turnips Acres (30)	Turnips Produce in Bushels (31)	Mangel Wurzel Acres (32)	Mangel Wurzel Produce in Bushels (33)	Carrots, bushels (34)	Beans, bushels (35)	Hops, lbs (36)	Hay, tons of 2000 lbs, or bundles of 16 lbs (37)	Clover Seed, Timothy Seed, or other Grass Seed, bushels (38)
10	230	7	495			1	30	2	400								40	
3	50	1	25					1	100									
½	36							½	40	¾	400						5	
6	100	5	200					1	200	3	1600	½	600	200			10	
5	100	2	50			¾	50	½	40	⅛	40	⅛	80	100			15	
5	100	4	70			1½	30	¾	60	¼	120	¼	150	170			15	
6	120	7	200					1	150								12	

Jonas Vollick, C 7 L1 m 99 acres total with 72 cultivated; 34 ¼ acres crops in 1860, 35 1/2 acres pasture, 2 acres of gardens, 27 acres woods, with cash value of the farm being $4000.00 and of farming implements being $35.00. 19 acres fall wheat, producing 436 bushels; 7 acres of spring wheat producing 90 bushesl, 5 acres of peas producing 100 bushels; 2 acres of oats producing 50 bushels; 3/4 acres of Indian Corn producing 50 bushels; 1/2 acre of pototates producing 40 bushels; 1/8 acre of turnips producing 40 bushels; 1/8 acre of mangel Wurtzel [field beet and fodder beet] producing 80 bushels, 100 bushels carrots, 15 tons of hay, 60 lbs wool, 30 yards of flannel

1865: Jonas Vollick a freeholder on Conc 7 Lot 1 East Flamborough Township. Joseph Vollick is on the same land with him and Wesley is on Conc 8 Lot 1

Abstract Index to Deeds C 7 L 1 East Flamborough Tp Wentworth Co.
Grantor Jonas Vollick to Samuel Newell S 1/2 of N. 1/2 50 acres B&S $3200.00
Instrument date 14 March 1866, Registration Date 20 March 1866

1871 Hamilton Wentworth Co. Census age 72 b. Ontario NC Germ. dist 23 p.13
BURIAL: Bethel Cemetery. Jonas is listed as Methodist, died of old age at 79 y, 6 mos.

His will signed 13 November 1873 provides bequests to
1. grandchildren Cornelis, Mary and Amanda, daughters of his late son Wesley to receive $100.00 to be invested and divided equally between them when they are 21.
2. Daughter-in-law Sarah Ann, widow of late son Joseph to receive $60.00
3. Rest of estate to sons James, Nelson and Morris and daughters Sophia, Amanda, Lovina and Esther, to be divided 2/3 to his sons and 1/3 to his daughters

The following 11 images are from the estate file of Jonas Vollick, Wentworth Surrogate Court, Hamilton. File #1226. Archives of Ontario GS1-603. Inventory 22-205

No 1226.
Surrogate Court
Wentworth

No 1226. +
Will of
Jonas Bollick
Gentleman

Probate granted 5 Febry
1877

Twenty seven days to
Frederic Norman
Executor &c

Reg in Lib. N. folio 306

In the goods of
Jonas Bollick
deceased

Application
received and filed
the 2d day of February
1877
J. A. Ghent
Registrar

In the Surrogate Court of the County of Wentworth

In the goods of
Jonas Dollick }
deceased }

I William Van Norman of the Township of
East Flamboro in the County of Wentworth
Yeoman make oath and say

1 That I am one of the Executors named in the
last Will and Testament of the said Jonas Dollick
deceased

2 That said deceased died on or about the
fifth day of January A.D. 1877 at the Township
of East Flamboro, and that said deceased at
the time of his death had a fixed place of abode
at the Township of East Flamboro in the said
County of Wentworth

3 That the personal Estate and effects of the said
deceased which he in any way died possessed of
or entitled to and for and in respect to which
probate of the said Will is to be granted are of
or about the value of Five hundred and fifty
dollars.

Sworn before me at the
City of Hamilton in the
County of Wentworth
this 2nd day of February
A.D. 1877.   }   William Van Norman

        A. Dewsnip
A Commissioner in B.R. &c
for County of Wentworth

Unto the Surrogate Court of the County of
Wentworth

The Petition of William Van Norman of the Town
ship of East Flamboro in the County of Wentworth
Yeoman and David Horning Binkley of the same
Township Yeoman

Sheweth -

That James Dallett late of the said Township of
East Flamboro Gentleman deceased died on or
about the fifth day of January A.D.1877 at East
Flamboro, and that said deceased at the time
of his death had a fixed place of abode at the
Township of East Flamboro in the said County
of Wentworth.

That the said deceased in his lifetime duly
made his last Will and Testament bearing date
the Thirteenth day of November A.D.1873

That your petitioners are two of the Executors
named in the said Will

That the personal Estate and effects of the
said deceased which he in any way died
possessed of or entitled to and for and in respect
of which probate of the said Will is to be granted
are of or about the value of Five hundred and fifty
dollars to the best of your petitioners knowledge and
belief

Wherefore your Petitioners pray that probate of the
said Will of the said deceased may be granted to
them by this Honorable Court.

Dated 2 February
A.D.1877

William Van Norman
David H. Binkley

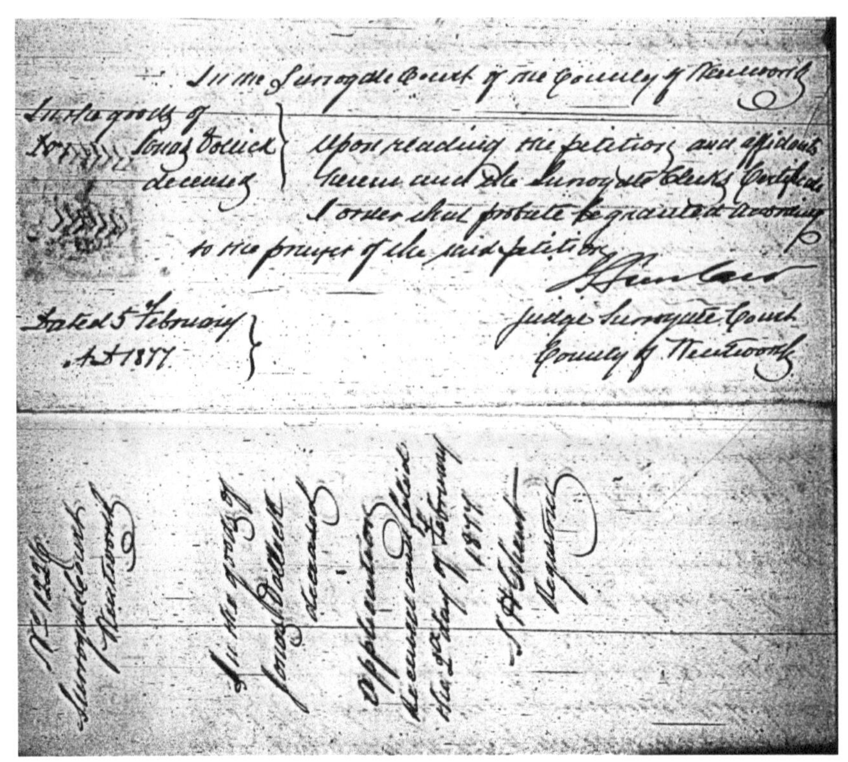

In the Surrogate Court of the County of Wentworth
In the goods of
Jonas Bollick
deceased
Upon reading the petition and affidavits
herein and the Surrogate Clerk's Certificate
I order that probate be granted according
to the prayer of the said petition
Judge Surrogate Court
County of Wentworth
Dated 5 February
A.D. 1877

IN THE SURROGATE COURT OF THE

County of Wentworth

In the Goods of *Jonas Vollick* — deceased.

I, *John Wesley Morden* of the *Township City of Hamilton* of *East Flam* in the County of *Wentworth Commission Merchant* make oath and say: —

That I knew *Jonas Vollick* late of the *Township* of *East Flamboro* in the County of *Wentworth Gentleman* deceased. —

That on or about the *Thirteenth* — day of *November* in the year of our Lord one thousand eight hundred and *seventy three* — I was present and did see the said *Jonas Vollick* sign and declare the paper writing hereunto annexed, as and for the last Will and Testament of the said *Jonas Vollick* —

That I, deponent and *Edward Pepper* of the said Township of East Flamboro Yeoman —

did subscribe our names as witnesses to the execution of the said Will at the request of the said Testat**or**, and in presence of each other *and in presence of the said Testator*; and lastly, that the several names subscribed as witnesses to the execution of the said Will are of the proper handwriting of this deponent and the said *Edward Pepper* — respectively.

And I further say that I verily believe that the said Testat**or** at the time of the execution of the said last Will and Testament was of sound and perfect mind, memory, and understanding.

Sworn before me at *the City of Hamilton* in the County of *Wentworth* this *second* day of *February* A.D. 187*7*

W. Sampier *John Wesley Morden*
A Commissioner in B&c
County of Wentworth

In the Surrogate Court of the *County* of

Wentworth

In the Goods of *Jonas Bollick* — deceased —

I, *David Horning Binkley* — of the *Township* of *East Flamboro* in the County of *Wentworth Yeoman* make oath and say that I believe this paper writing hereto prefixed and marked "A," contains the true and original last Will and Testament of *Jonas Bollick* — late of the *Township* — of *East Flamboro* — in the County of *Wentworth Gentleman* That I am *one of the* Executors therein named, and that I will faithfully administer the personal estate and effects of the said Testator, by paying his just debts, and the legacies contained in his Will, so far as the same will thereunto extend, and the law bind me; and that I will exhibit a true and perfect inventory of all and singular the personal estate and effects, rights and credits of the Testator, and render a just and full account of my Executorship whenever required by law so to do.

Sworn at *the City of Hamilton,* in the County of *Wentworth* the *second* day of *February* A.D. 1877 before me

David H. Binkley

R. W. Dancker

A Commissioner in B.R. &c., in and for the County of, *Wentworth*

OATH OF EXECUTOR.

In the Surrogate Court of the *County of Wentworth*

In the Goods of *Jonas Bollick* — deceased

I, *William Van Norman* — of the *Township* of *East Flamboro* — in the County of *Wentworth Yeoman* make oath and say that I believe this paper writing hereto prefixed and marked "A," contains the true and original last Will and Testament of *Jonas Bollick* — late of the *Township* of *East Flamboro* — in the County of *Wentworth Gentleman* — That I am *one of the* Executors therein named, and that I will faithfully administer the personal estate and effects of the said Testator, by paying his just debts, and the legacies contained in his Will, so far as the same will thereunto extend, and the law bind me; and that I will exhibit a true and perfect inventory of all and singular the personal estate and effects, rights and credits of the Testator, and render a just and full account of my Executorship whenever required by law so to do.

Sworn at *the City of Hamilton,*
in the County of *Wentworth* the
second day of *February* A.D. 187*7*
before me

William Van Norman

A Commissioner in B.R. &c., in and for the County of *Wentworth*

A

I Jonas Vollick of the Township of East Flamboro in
the County of Wentworth and province of Ontario. Gentleman
being of sound and disposing mind Memory and understanding
do make publish and declare this to be my last will and
Testament hereby revoking and making null and void
all former last wills and testaments and writings in the
nature of last wills and testaments by me heretofore made
My Will is first that my funeral charges and just debts
shall be paid by my Executors herein after named

The residue of my property which shall not be required
for the payment of my just debts funeral charges and the
expenses attending the execution of this my will. I give and
bequeathe as follows, To Wit:

1st. I give and bequeath to my Grandchildren, Cornelia. Mary.
and Amanda Vollick daughters of my late son Wesley
Vollick the sum of One hundred dollars the said sum I direct
my executors to put to Interest and when the youngest of the
said Grand children arrives at the full age of Twenty one years to
divide the amount equally between them share and share alike

2nd. I give and bequeath to my daughter in law Sarah Ann Vollick.
widow of my late son Joseph Vollick the sum of Sixty dollars
to be paid by my executors as soon after my decease as may be
convenient

3d. The residue of my personal (and if any real) estate at my decease I
give and bequeath to my sons named — James. Nelson. and Morris
Vollick and my daughters named. Sophia, Amanda. Levina and
Esther Vollick in the following proportions that is to say Two
thirds to be equally divided between my said sons and one third
to be equally divided between my said daughters. And I
wish it to be understood that it is my will that the above named
legacies regarding my own Children shall be paid according to
age the oldest first and so on until all have received his
and her share as above directed

And I do nominate and appoint my son in law. William
Hannaman and my friends David Horning Binkley and
Horatio Nelson Morden Executors of this my last will and Testament

In witness whereof I the said Jonas Vollick have hereunto subscribed
my name and affixed my seal this Thirteenth day of November
in the year of our Lord one thousand eight hundred and seventy three

Jonas ^{his} ✕ Vollick
mark

Signed sealed and declared by the said Jonas Vollick to be his last
will and testament in presence of Edward Pepper and
John Wesley Morden who at his request and in his presence
have subscribed their names as witnesses hereto in presence
of each other

Edward Pepper
John W. Morden

This is the last Will and Testament of Jonas Vollick
late of the Township of East Flamboro Yeoman
deceased referred to in the annexed affidavits

William Van Norman
David H. Binkley

At Dundas
A Commissioner
in B R & County
of Wentworth

Last Will and Testament of Jonas Vollick

Filed 2nd February 1877

OFFICE OF THE SURROGATE CLERK.

In the goods of *Jonas Vollick*

deceased, named in a certain Notice of Application for a grant of Probate

dated the *2d* day of *February*

A.D., 187*6* as late of the *Township* of *East Flamboro'* in the

County of *Wentworth Gentleman*

I, SIR JAMES LUKIN ROBINSON, the Surrogate Clerk, do hereby certify that no Notice of Application in respect of the Goods of the said deceased, has been received by me from any of the Registrars of the Surrogate Courts (in Ontario) save the above, from the Surrogate Court for the

County of *Wentworth*

grant of Probate of the Will bearing date the *13th* day of *November* A.D., 187*3*.

And I further certify, that no Caveat or copy of Caveat, against the grant of Probate or Administration on the Goods of the deceased, has been lodged with or received by me.

Dated the *3rd* day of *February* A.D., 187*6*

To

The Registrar of the Surrogate Court of the

County of *Wentworth*

Hamilton

James L. Robinson

Surrogate Clerk.

Jonas Vollick and Mary Gilbert were married before 1823 in Ontario.They had the following children:

i. James Gilbert Vollick was born on 23 Jan 1823 in Halton Co. Ontario. He died on 18 May 1896 in Rawdon, Hastings Co. Ontario.

ii. Sophia Jane Vollick was born on 28 May 1825 in Upper Canada. She married Thomas Tansley before 1843. She died on 25 Jul 1888 in Burford, Brant Co. Ontario.

iii. Nelson Vollick was born about 1828 in Nelson Township Halton Co. Ontario. He died on 15 May 1879 in Carrick Township Bruce Co. Ontario.

iv. Amanda Melissa Vollick was born on 19 Jan 1829 in E. Flamborough Twp, Wentworth Co. Ontario. She died on 22 Jun 1910 in Hamilton, Wentworth Co. Ontario.

v. Morris Vollick was born on 12 Feb 1831 in Nelson Tp, Halton Co. Upper Canada. He married Mary Kemp on 12 Apr 1860 in Bruce Co. Ontario. He died on 08 Jul 1890 in Carrick Township Bruce Co. Ontario.

vi. William Wesley (Wesley) Vollick was born on 12 Mar 1833 in Upper Canada. He married Maria Jane Whitfield on 23 Apr 1857 in Belnap's Hotel, Hamilton, Wentworth Co Ontario. He died on 28 Jun 1866 in Kilbride, Halton Co. Ontario.

vii. Livinia (Lovina) C. Vollick was born in Mar 1834 in Hamilton, Ontario. She married James Davidson in 1852 in Ontario. She died on 18 Jan 1914 in Cook Co. Illinois.

viii. Joseph Morris Vollick was born on 29 Dec 1836 in Upper Canada. He married Sarah Ann Marical on 04 Mar 1858 in Waterdown, East Flamborough Township. He died on 10 Jun 1869 in Kilbride, Nelson Township Halton Co. Ontario.

ix. Hestor (Estor Mary) Vollick was born about 1842 in Upper Canada. She married Francis William Mills on 04 Oct 1859 in East Flamborough Township Halton Co. Ontario. She died after 1880 possibly in St. Clair, Michigan

Matthias Vollick & Catherine Burkholder

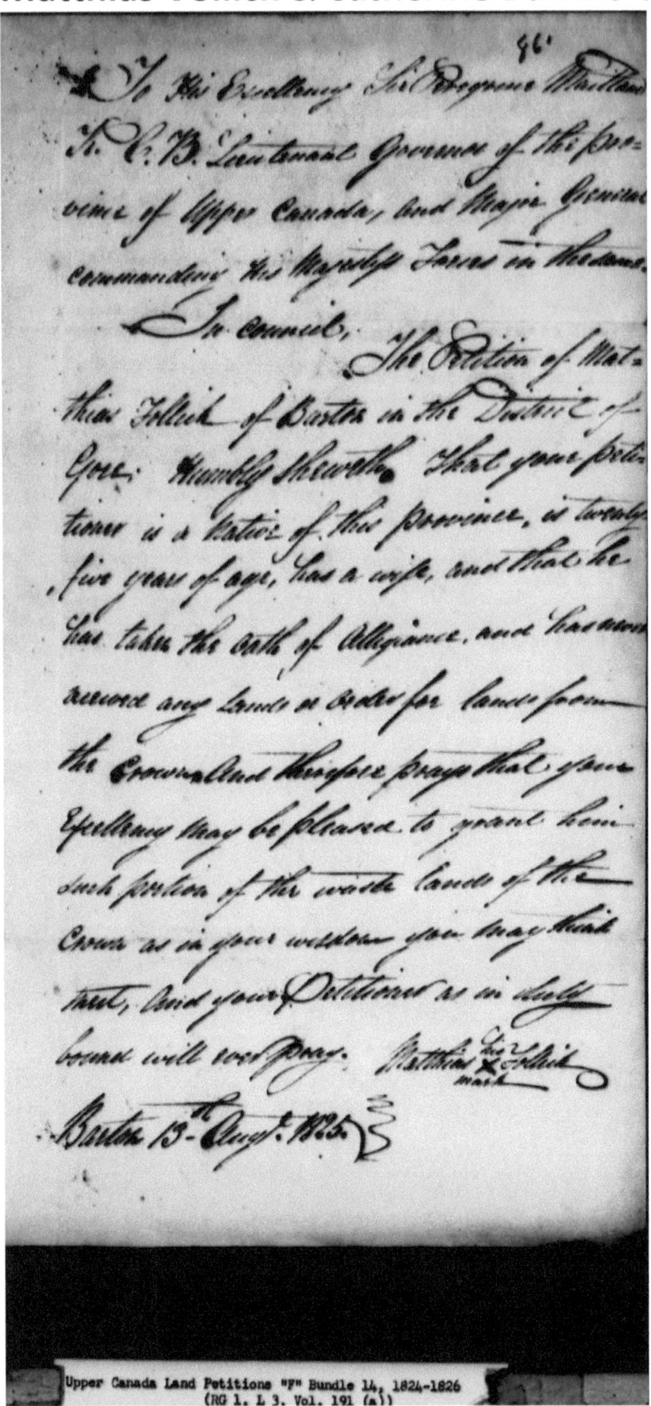

In March 1825 Matthias Vollick submitted a petition which states that Matthias Folluk [sic] of Barton in the District of Gore, married and 25 years of age, has taken the Oath of Allegiance, has never received any lands and now requests a grant of land

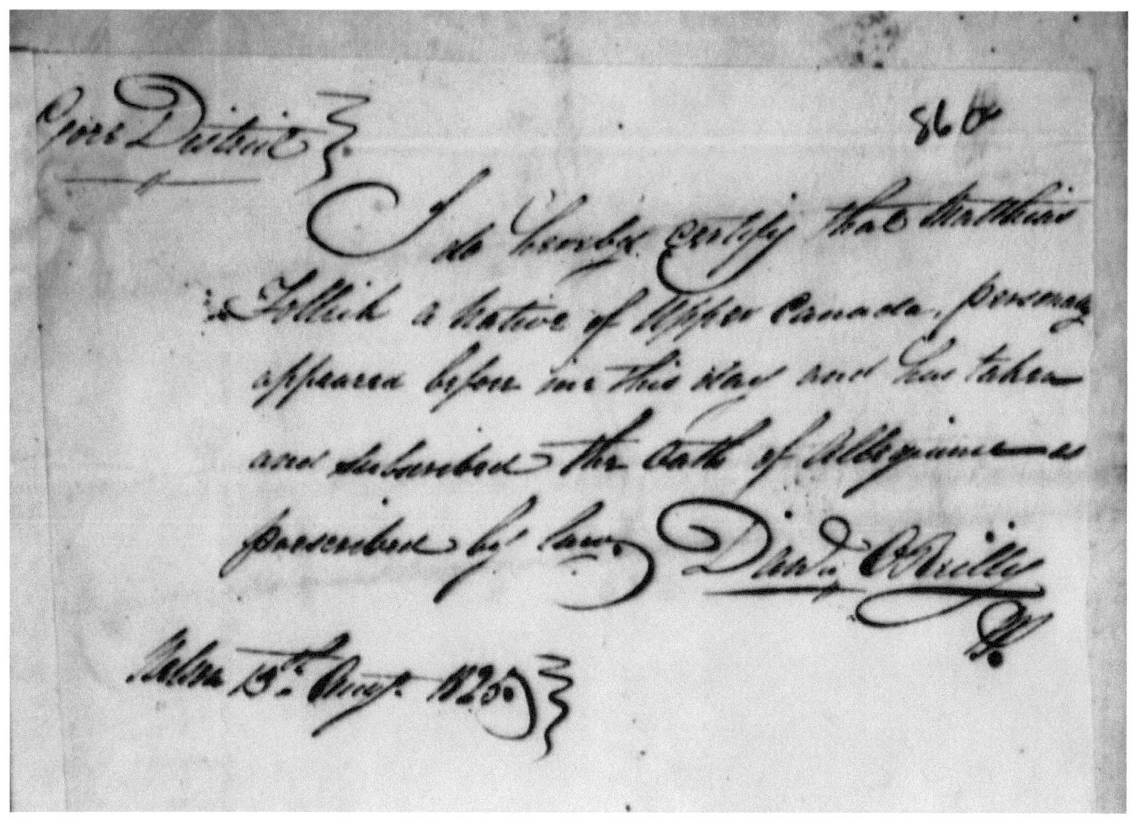

In August as part of that same Petition (#86) he presents an affidavit stating that *"Matthias Follick is a native of Upper Canada"* and has appeared to take the Oath of Allegiance.

South   March 18th 1825

I Do Certify that Cornelious Volick and Mathias Volick have allways been Loyal Subyects and did do their duty well under me the late war and are good honest Peaceable men

Captain Henry Pawling
First Regiment
Lincoln Militia

Capt. Henry Pawling of the First Regiment of the Lincoln Militia signs an affidavit that both Cornelius Volick and Matthias Volick have been loyal subjects and *"did their duty well under me"* in the late war (War of 1812)

The question arises whether Cornelius refers to Matthias' father or was there another brother named Cornelius who has not been found?

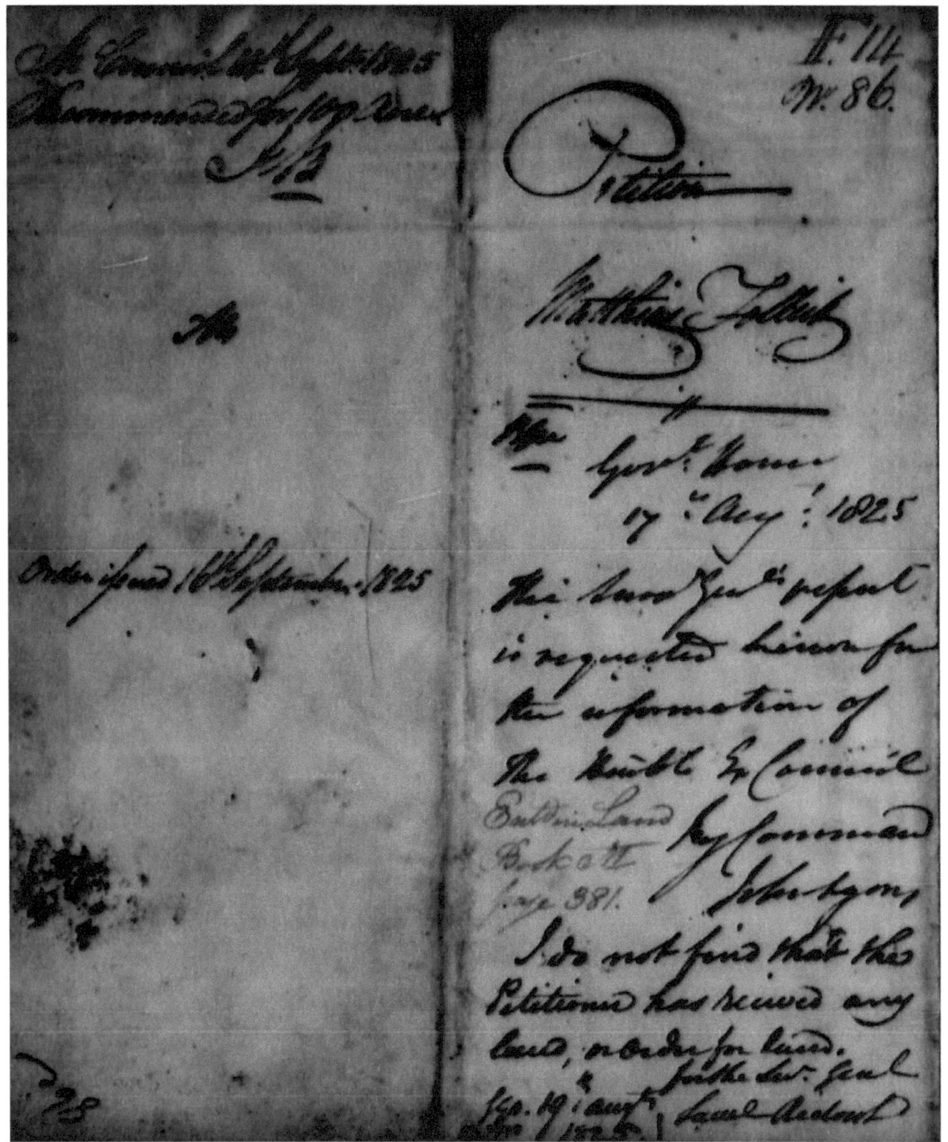

It appears Matthias was granted his request for land for a faded notation on the envelope of his petition reads *"Entered in Land Book (unable to decipher the letter of the Land Book, possibly "M") on page 381"* When land was granted an entry was made in the Land Books.

Nov. 14, 1825: Barton Township
Township Papers, Nelson, MS 658 Reel # 334 Page 310

Chippawa February 29th 1840

Dear Sir,
One Mathias Follick has been to me to get a deed out for him he say that it is his name that appears for west half of 14 in the 4th Concession of the Township of Nelson Gore District. I wish you to inform me what the reasons is that the deed is stopped or what entitled him to the location either from Flank ensign? or a settler, this Mathias Follick

has resided in this neighbourhood for sometime. I will be a Toronto by the 10th of March and I trust you will have Cook & Sleight Deeds ready and you will please to mention to Mr. Lee that I am ?? he should get on with the Peter Coleman ? deed for land in ??your atention will oblige you ?? G McMicking John Redenhurst Esquire Surveryor General Office [19]

A check of the Computerized Ontario Land Index shows that Matthias Follick of Barton received this lot 4 September 1825 as a Free Grant but had to pay Full Fees.

Pte. Matthew FOLICK, Age from 19 yrs. to 39 yrs. inc., Line #16, 10th Coy., 2nd Regt. Lincoln Militia. LIMITS: Stamford, Thorold and Pelham. DATED: 1828 or 1829.

1830 census Nelson Township Gore District: We find Matthias Volk [sic] living beside Jacob Burkholder. The top part of the page is missing - approximately 14 names lost. Matthias is shown as having one male over 16 yrs., 1 female over 16 and 2 females under 16 for a total of 4 family members.

1838: living Hespeler, Ont.

1851:Puslinch Township, Wellington Co. [census p.11]

	Name	Occupation	Born	Religion	Age
10	[Serguen] Sarker	Labourer	Canada	No religion	17
11	Matthias Follick	Farmer	Canada	New Connexion Methodist	58
12	Cathrine Follick	Wife	"	"	43
13	Mary Follick	Daughter	" "	" "	23
14	Hanna Follick	" "	" "	" "	21
15	Catherine Follick	" "	" "	" "	13
16	Sarah Follick	" "	" "	" "	7
17	Martha Follick	" "	" "	" "	5
18	Emela Follick	" "	" "	" "	3
19	Joseph Follick	Sons Labourer	" "	" "	20
20	David Follick	" "	" "	" "	17
21	Enoch Follick	" "	" "	" "	15
22	William Follick	" "	" "	" "	10

Puslinch Township Land
F1 Lot 1
South Half: 1856 letter indicates Mathias Follick was on the north part of the south half

The 1861 census finds Matthias in Hay Township, Huron County

	Name	Occupation	Birthplace		Religion		Age
16	Matthias Follick	Farmer	✓ U. Canada		N. C.	✓	62
17	Catharine Follick		"		"	✓	52
18	David Follick		"		"	✓	26
19	Catharine Follick		"		"	U. Canada	23
20	William Follick		"		"	✓	19
21	Sarah Follick		"		"	✓	17
22	Martha Jane Follick		"		"	✓	15
23	Caroline Follick		"		"	✓	13
24	Henry Follick		"		"	✓	26

Matthias died 11 January 1870 in Goderich, Huron County and is buried in Hillsgreen Cemetery

Matthias Follick and Catharine Burkholder were married before Sep 1826.They had the following children:

i. Elizabeth Follick was born on 12 Sep 1826 in Ontario. She married Joseph Rife on 25 Sep 1845 in Puslinch Township Wellington Co. Ontario. She died on 18 Apr 1877 in Hay Tp Huron Co. Ontario.

ii. E. Mary (Mary) Follick was born about 1828 in Ontario. She married George Parker before 1860. She died on 31 May 1883 in Hay Township Huron Co. Ontario.

iii. Hannah Follick was born about 1830 in Ontario. She died in 1860.

iv. Joseph Follick was born on 07 Jul 1832 in Hamilton, Barton Township Wentworth Co. Ontario. He married Mary McLean on 16 May 1860 in Clarke Township Durham Co. Ontario. He died on 15 Apr 1907 in Niagara Falls, Welland Co. Ontario.

v. David Follick was born on 07 Mar 1835 in Waterloo, Ontario. He married Margaret (Samantha?) Shuart about 1863. He died on 11 May 1909 in Hensall, Hay Township Huron Co. Ontario.

vi. Enoch Follick was born on 08 Aug 1836 in Ontario. He married Ann Fenwick in 1859. He died on 25 Jan 1913 in Exeter, Hay Township Huron Co. Ontario.

vii. Catherine Follick was born in Mar 1839 in Hespeler Ontario. She married William Fenwick in 1861. She died after 1900 in California.

viii. William Vollick was born on 24 Jun 1844 in Waterloo, Ontario. He died on 26 May 1922 in Hamilton, Barton Township Wentworth Co. Ontario.

ix. Sarah Ann Follick was born on 30 Jun 1844 in Hespeler Ontario. She married Justus Mellick on 23 Nov 1865 in Huron Co. Ontario. She died on 09 May 1923 in Hensall, Huron County Ontario.

x. Martha Jane Follick was born on 17 Jul 1846 in Hespeler Ontario. She married Charles Whiteman on 01 Jul 1873 in Huron Co. Ontario. She died on 21 Dec 1915 in Detroit, Wayne Co. Michigan.

xi. Emma Follick was born in 1848 in Hespeler Ontario. She married John Fenwick on 26 Apr 1871 in Huron Co. Ontario.

Mary Vollick & Albert Bradt

I suggest Mary is another child of Cornelius and Eve (Larroway) Vollick. Her 1801 date of birth fits with other known children. Her place of birth, Louth, fits with Cornelius's location, who was still living near St. Catharines at the time.

In the 1818 Assessment Nelson Township Gore District Cornelius Follick [sic] is living beside Isaac Bradt and Albert Bradt. In October 1819 Albert petitioned for land in Nelson Township.

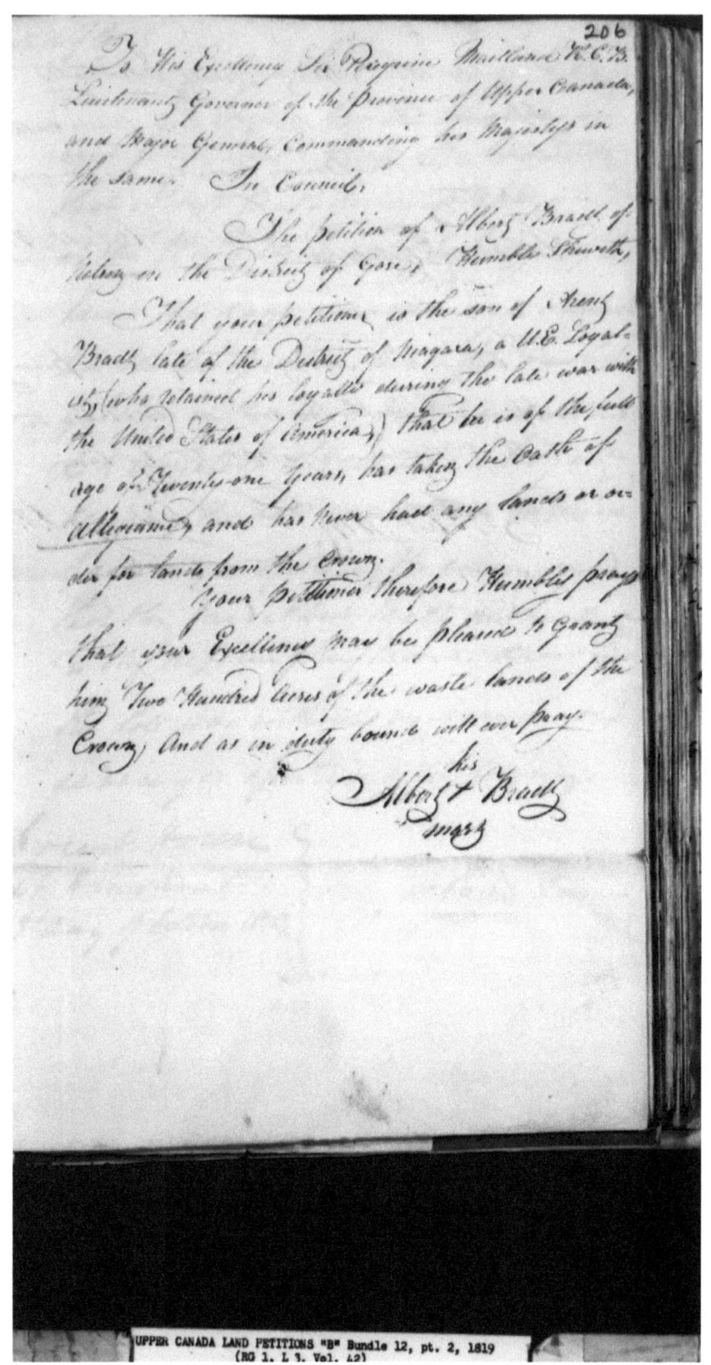

To His Excellency Sir Peregrine Maitland K.C.B &c.
Lieutenant Governor of the Province of Upper Canada,
and Major General, Commanding his Majesty's in
the same. In Council.

The petition of Albert Bradt of
Nelson in the District of Gore, Humbly Sheweth,

That your petitioner is the son of Arent
Bradt, late of the District of Niagara, a U.E. Loyalist, (who retained his loyalty during the late war with
the United States of America,) that he is of the full
age of Twenty one Years, has taken the Oath of
Allegiance, and has never had any lands or order for lands from the Crown.

Your petitioner therefore Humbly prays
That your Excellency may be pleased to Grant
him Two Hundred Acres of the waste lands of the
Crown, And as in duty bound will ever pray.

his
Albert + Bradt
mark

Petition 206 October 29, 1819

206a

I certify that Albert Bradt personally
appeared before me this day and made oath
that he is the person described in the within
Petition
Nelson 29th Octr 1819   Danl. O'Reilly J.P.

I certify that Albert Bradt of Nelson personally
appeared before me this day and has taken the
Oath of Allegiance &c as presented by law
Nelson 29th Octr 1819   Danl. O'Reilly J.P.

District of Gore }

206 b

We James Brooks Chairman and George Rolph Clerk of the same hereby Certify that Albert Nash personally appeared at the General Quarter Sessions of the peace this day is recognized by the Magistrates to be the son of Aaron Nash of the Township of Nelson in the said District an enrolled UE Loyalist who retained his Loyalty during the late war without suspicion of aiding or assisting the enemy and that the said Albert Nash did his duty in the defence of the Province during the late war without suspicion of aiding or assisting the enemy.

Court House at Hamilton this 19th day of October 1819. }

Jas. Brooks Chairman

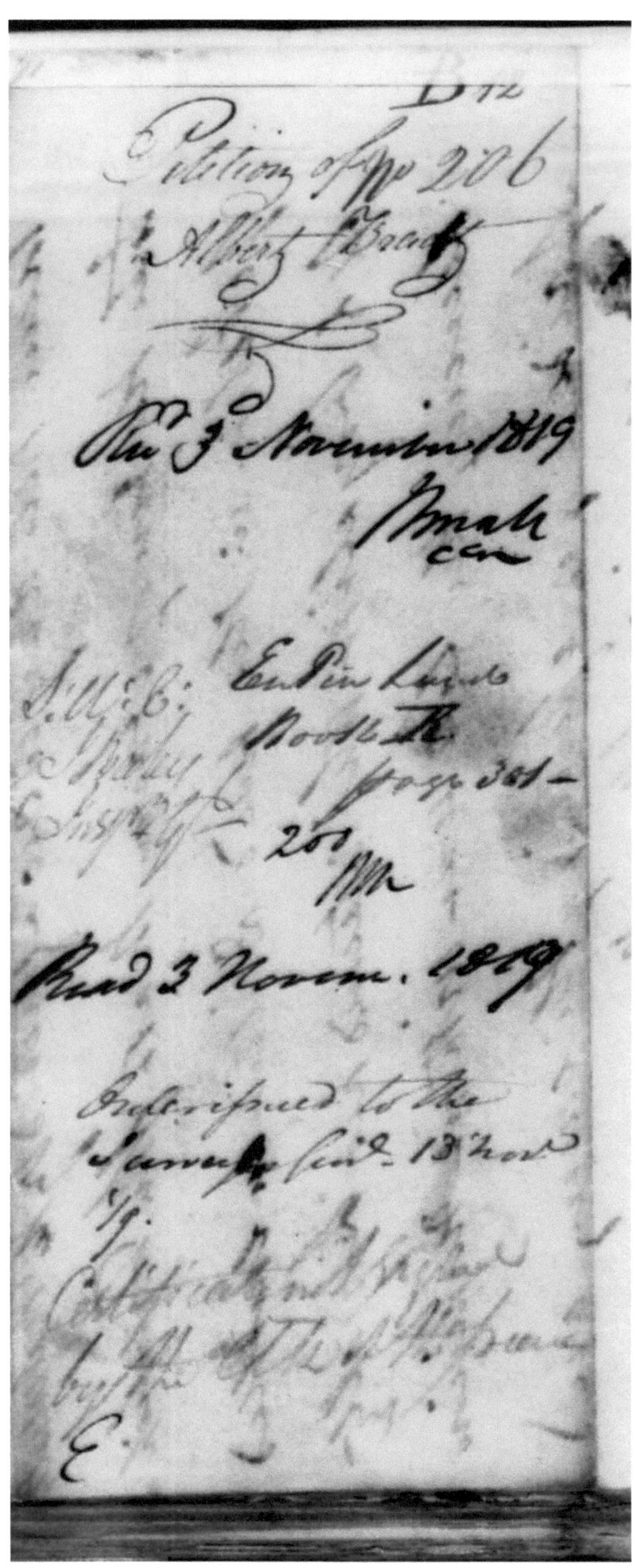

Albert's land was granted and entered in Land Book K on page 301.

In 1824 Albert petitioned again for land in Nelson Township. He stated he was 33 years old, married with 5 children and had been in Upper Canada for about 30 years.

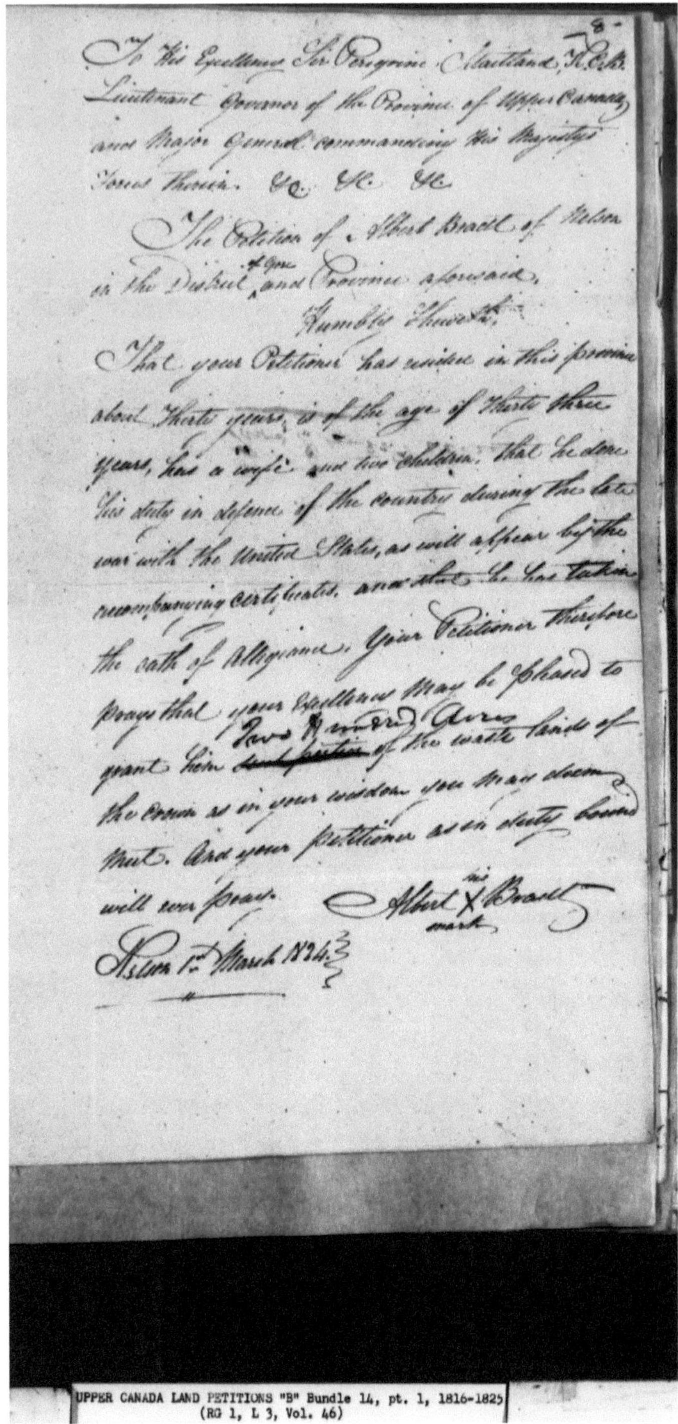

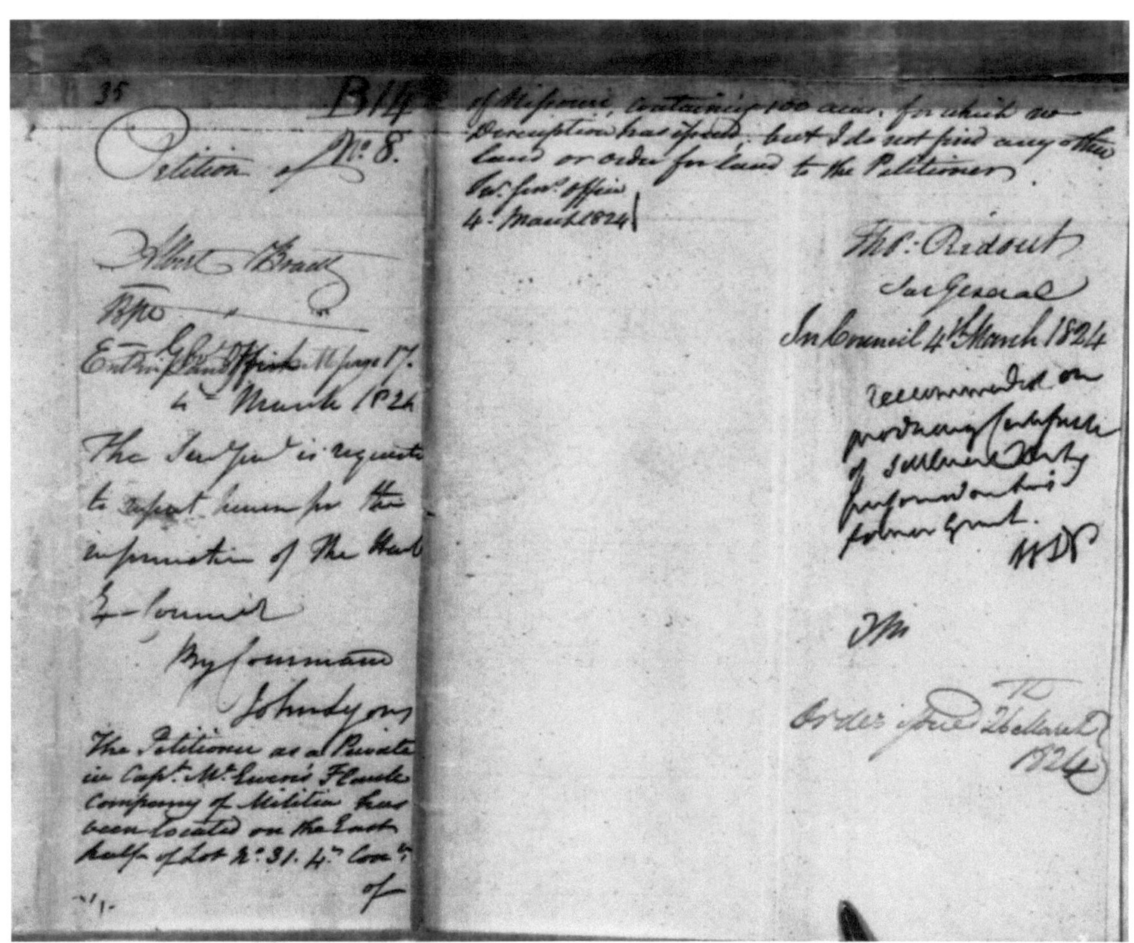

1851 Census Part 2, Nelson Tp Halton Co.

9	Albert Bradt	Farmer	New York	Baptist			X	61
10	Mary Bradt	Housekeeper	" Can	"			X	51
11	Eliza Jane "		"	"				23
12	Sylvester "	Lab.	"	"				19
13	Lusia Ann "		"	"				15
14	Mary Cath "		"	"				11
15	Andrew Coffer	Lab -	Ireland					15
16	Mary Elizabeth "		" Can					4

Obituary (in Christian Messenger of 8 Jan 1857?):

At husband's home, Mrs. Mary BRATT, age 55 years, 4 months 2 days, wife of Albert BRATT, Nelson Township on 13 Dec 1856, born in Louth on 1 Aug. 1801, parents were Presbyterian. Married at 24 years.

Brandt [sic], Albert, 1858 Tremaine Map, Nelson Tp, Halton Co. Conc 4 Lot 4

Bradt, Albert Living in Nelson Township, 1861,page 86

	Name	Occupation	Place of Birth	Religion		Age
32	Albert Bradt	Farmer	U.S	Baptist	✓	70
33	Daniel Bradt	do	U.C.	B	✓	33
34	Silvester Bradt	do	U.C	B	✓	28
35	Eliza Bradt		U.C.	B	✓	31
36	Elsa A Bradt		U.C.	B	✓	24
37	Mary Bradt		U.C	B	✓	20
38	George Bradt		U.C	B	✓	10
39	Dianah Bradt		U.C	B	✓	7
40	Elizabeth Bradt		U.C.	B	✓	13

Bradt, Albert Living in Nelson Township, 1871, division 2, page 29

Name		Sex	Age		Country	Religion	Origin	Occupation	
Bradt	Albert	M	80	—	U.S.	Baptist	German American	Farmer	W
"	Daniel	M	43	—	O	"	"	"	W
"	Eliza J.	F	41	—	"	"	"	—	—
"	Elsa	F	33	—	"	"	"	—	—
"	Mary C.	F	29	—	"	"	"	—	—
"	George C.	M	19	—	"	"	"	Farmer	—

Albert died of dropsy on 19 April 1878 in Nelson Township at the age of 86.

Albert Bradt and Mary Vollick had the following children:

i. Elizabeth Maria Bradt was born ca 1817 in Ontario. She died on 09 Mar 1888 in Nelson Township Halton Co Ontario.

ii. Magdalene Bradt was born in 1823. She died on 15 Dec 1903.

iii. Eliza Jane Bradt was born about 1827 in Ontario.

iv. Daniel Bradt was born about 21 Apr 1828. He died on 23 Nov 1914 in Nelson Tp Halton Co Ontario.

v. Sylvester Bradt was born about 1831 in Ontario.

vi. Laura Ann Bradt was born about 1835 in Ontario.

vii. Mary Catherine Bradt was born on 28 May 1840 in Nelson Tp, Halton Co. Ontario. She died on 25 Mar 1923 in Nelson Tp, Halton Co. Ontario.

viii. Mary Elizabeth Bradt was born about 1847 in Ontario.

Peter Vollick & Nancy Hanart

In March 1824 Peter petitioned for land in Nelson Township Halton County. The envelope for his petition indicates he received the land and details were recorded in Land Book K.

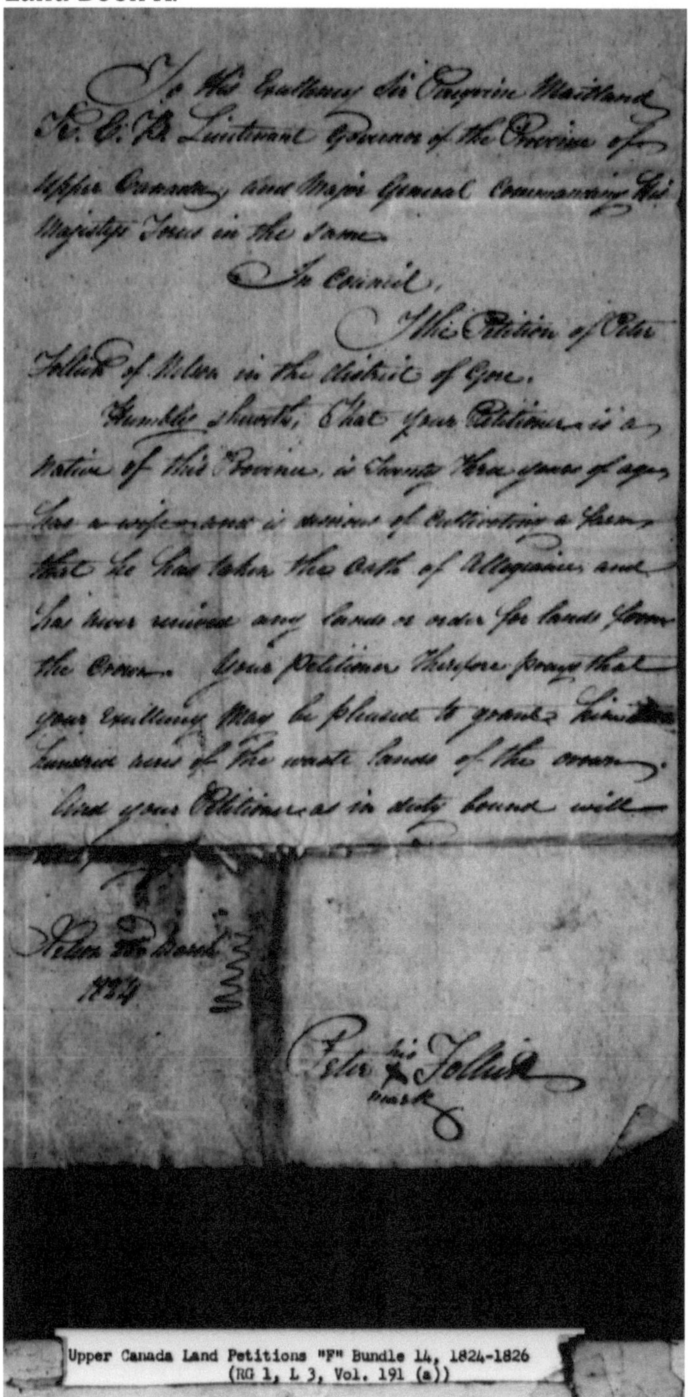

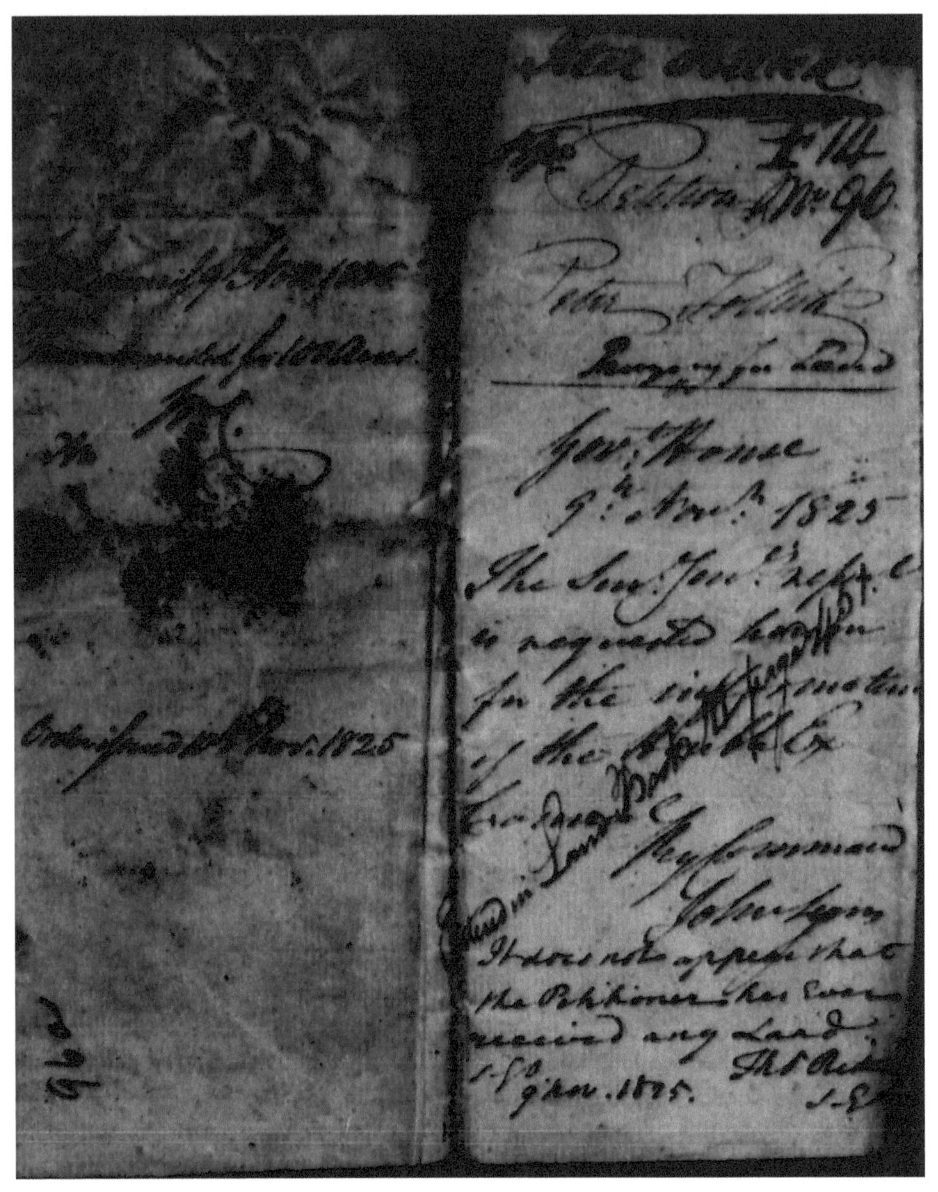

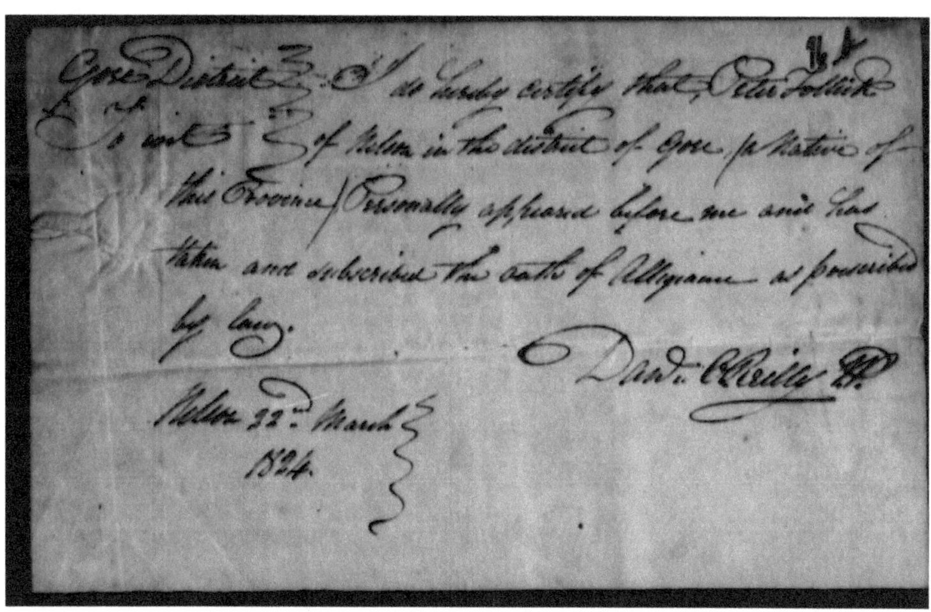

Township Papers, Nelson, MS 658 Reel# 334
Page 234
District of York
Personally came before me Hugh Willson Esquire one of his Majesties Justices of the
Peace in and for said District Peter Follick and Jonas Follick both of the Nelson in said
district yeoman. Who being duly sworn deposeth and saith that the streets front and
near of Lot Number one in the fourth Concession of Nelson, New Survey is cleared out
two rods wide the whole width of said lot, and that there is ten acres well choped out
for growing wheat withn fence, and a House sixteen by twenty feet in the clear built
and said lot. Sworn and subscribed before me this second day of June 1824.

Peter X Follick
Jonas X Follick
Hugh Willson J.P.

—

J. Baley

In the 1851 census we find his son Peter, age 10 living in Trafalgar Tp Halton County
with the Scriver family. His 12 year old daughter Eve is found with the Deforest
family in Nelson Township. I find no trace of Peter or his wife Nancy.

Peter Vollick and Nancy Hanart were married before 1830.They had the following
children:

i. Cornelius Vollick was born on 05 Jun 1830 in Nelson Township Halton Co. Ontario.
He married Elizabeth Catherine Charlotte Wilson before 1854. He died on 19 Jul
1912 in Attercliffe Station, Moulton Township Haldimand Co. Ontario.

ii. James Gilbert Vollick was born on 07 Feb 1833 in Nelson Township Halton Co. Ontario. He married Catherine McLean on 20 Nov 1859 in Haldimand Co. Ontario. He died on 20 Sep 1897 in N. Cayuga Township, Haldimand Co. Ontario.

iii. Agnes Vollick was born between 1836-1845 in Nelson Township, Halton Co. Ontario. She married Robert Finley Grier on 18 Feb 1869 in Waterdown, Nelson Tp, Halton Co Ontario. She died after 1881.

iv. Eve Vollick was born about 1839 in Ontario. She married Sam Ruddy on 18 Feb 1863 in East Flamborough Township Wentworth Co. Ontario. She died on 02 May 1902 in Nelson Tp, Halton Co. Ontario.

v. Peter Vollick was born about 1843 in Nelson Township Halton County Ontario. He married Charlotte Lovina (Vina) Barclay on 30 Apr 1865 in Wentworth Co. Ontario. He died between 1883-1894.

Janine Vollick & Jacob Burkholder

1830 census Nelson Township Gore District shows Jacob Burkholder living beside Matthias Volk [sic] who is married to Jacob's sister Catherine. Jacob is shown as being head of a family of 3 consisting of himself and wife, plus one daughter under the age of 16.

On 12 Dec. 1832 Jacob purchased 75 acres NW half L1 C 4 Nelson Township NS from James Cleaver for 150 pounds. Witness David Burkholder Sr. On 30 Apr. 1836 he sold 22 acres of this land to B. McCay. On 21 Jan 1843 he sold 2 acres of this land to William Smith-Kenny.

In the 1842 census for Nelson Township Gore District Jacob Burkholder is shown as having 9 children. He is neighbours to the following men: Albert Bradt (married to Mary Vollick); Richard Vollick (m. to Elizabeth Burkholder); David Burkholder (married to Margaret Vollick); George Vollick; W. Bradt.

In 1842 Jacob is the head of a family of 11, all natives of Canada. He has 1 male under 5, 1 female under 5, 5 males ages 5 to 14 and 2 females ages 5 to 14 in his family. He is listed as married age 30-60, his wife as married age 14-45.

Janine died before May 1848

Jacob Burkholder and Janine Vollick were married before 1830.They had the following children:

i. daughter Burkholder was born about 1830. (as per the 1830 Census of Nelson Township)s

ii. Henry M. Burkholder was born about 1831 in Nelson Township Halton Co. Ontario.

iii. Isaac Cornelius Burkholder was born about 1831 in Nelson Township Halton Co. Ontario. He married Maryette F. before 1860. He died in 1933.

iv. Jacob Burkholder was born about 1832.

v. George Burkholder was born about 1834.

vi. Eliza Ann Burkholder was born on 13 Jun 1834 in Lowville, Halton Co. Ontario. She died on 26 Jul 1917 in Columbia, Tuscola, MI.

vii. Joseph Burkholder was born about 1835 in Nelson Township Halton Co. Ontario. He died on 25 Apr 1890 in East Nissouri Township Oxford Co. Ontario.

viii.Hannah C. Burkholder was born about 1838 in Nelson Township Halton Co. Ontario. She died on 04 Sep 1878 in Malahide, Elgin Co. Ontario.

ix. Martha Jane Burkholder was born about 1839 in Ontario. She died on 31 May 1926 in Elgin Co. Ontario.

x. Elizabeth Melvine Burkholder was born on 01 Sep 1844 in Nelson Township Halton Co. Ontario. She died on 04 Mar 1925 in Aylmer, Malahide, Elgin Co. Ontario.

xi. Elsie Burkholder was born about 1846 in Nelson Township Halton Co. Ontario. She died on 25 May 1871.

Eliza Vollick & Richard Lightheart & Jacob Burkholder

Eliza married Richard Lightheart on 4 March 1844 in Nelson Township, Halton County. [20] He died before 1848. Jacob Burkholder married his second wife Eliza Vollick (Janine's sister) on 09 May 1848.

1851 Nelson Township census: He is a farmer, Baptist. Living with him was Jacob Burkholder born 1832 and George Burkholder born 1834 , both shown as non-family members. Here he is married to his second wife, Janine Vollick's sister Eliza.

1851 Census Part 2, Nelson Tp Halton Co.

No.	Name		Occupation						Age
21	Jacob	Burkholder	Farmer	"	"	"		X	42
22	Eliza	Burkholder	Housekeeper	"	"	"		X	32
23	Isaac	"	B Smith	"	"	"			22
24	Henry	"	Lab	"	"	"			30
25	Eliza A	"		"	"	"			18
26	Hannah	"		"	"	"			14
27	Joseph	"		"	"	"			16
28	Martha	"		"	"	"			12
29	Elizabeth	"		"	"	"			7
30	Lucy	"		"	"	"			5
31	Phebe N	"		"	"	"			2
32	Jacob	"	Laborer	"	"	"			19
33	George	"	"	"	"	"			17

1858 Tremaine Map: Nelson Township Halton Co. New Survey, Conc. 4, Lot 1 is Jacob Burkholder

1859: sold remainder of land to Thomas Collings.

1871 North Cayuga Haldimand County census

	Surname	Name	Sex	Age						
81	Burkholder	Jacob	M	66	—		0		Baptist	German
	"	Eliza	F	52	—		"		"	"
	"	Joseph	M	34	—		"		"	"
	"	Hannah	F	32	—		"		"	"
	"	Phebe	F	20	—		"		"	"
	"	Rebecca	F	18	—		"		"	"
	"	Lydia	F	16	—		"		"	"
	"	Sarah	F	14	—		"		"	"

1881 Census East Nissouri Township, Oxford Co. p. 13

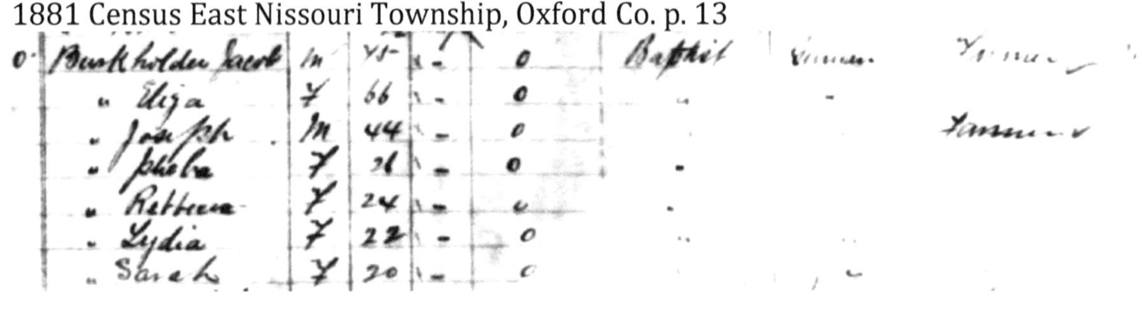

1891 Census Malahide, Elgin County

Eliza died 05 Jun 1892 in Malahide Township, Elgin County. Jacob died in 1894 and is buried Luton Cemetery, C 5 L 15 Malahide Township Elgin Co.

Jacob Burkholder and Eliza Follick were married on 09 May 1848. They had the following children:

i. Phoebe Rosilla Burkholder was born about 1849 in Nelson Tp Halton Co. Ontario. She died on 03 Jun 1921 in Malahide, Elgin Co. Ontario.

ii. Rebecca Matilda Burkholder was born about 1853. She died in 1938 in Malahide, Elgin Co. Ontario.

iii. Tilla Burkholder was born about 1855.

iv. Lydia Burkholder was born about 1856. She died on 12 Jul 1928 in Malahide, Elgin Co. Ontario.

v. Sarah Jemima Burkholder was born about 1857 in Nelson Tp Halton Co. Ontario. She died on 17 Dec 1933 in Malahide, Elgin Co. Ontario.

Richard Vollick & Elizabeth Burkholder

In the 1842 census for Nelson Township Gore District we find Richard Volick [sic] followed by David Burkholder (married to Margaret Vollick], George Volick; W. Bradt [I have not attempted to place him in the extensive Bradt family who were cousins to my Vollick family - there was also Albert Bradt [married to Richard's sister Mary] 6 names prior to Richard Volick on this census]; Jacob Burkholder [who married first Janine Vollick and then in 1848 Eliza Vollick Lightheart] Very nearby is Isaac Vollick (who married Sophia Burkholder, another sibling to David Burkholder and Elizabeth Burkholder]

Pte. Richard Volick, Age 19 yrs., Line #122, 2nd Regt. Gore Militia.
Pte. Jas. Volick, Age 26 yrs., Line #123, 2nd Regt. Gore Militia.
Pte. John Volick, Age 22 yrs., Line #124, 2nd Regt. Gore Militia.
Limits: Trafalgar, Nelson & the two Flamboroughs. Dated: 22nd Dec'r. 1828.

1842 Census of Nelson Township Gore District:
Richard Vollick, farmer, with 8 natives of Canada. He had 1 male under 5, 1 female under 5, 2 males ages 5 to 14, 1 female aged 5 to 14, one married age 30 to 60, one single age 30 to 60 and one married age 14 to 45. This agrees with his five children David, Levina, Isaac, Henry and Sarah.

He is found on Conc 8 Lot 1 on 100 acres, East Flamborough with Jonas Vollick on Conc 7 Lot 1.

Richard is in the 1851 agricultural census for East Flamborough Township living Conc 8, Lot 1 on 100 acres. He is on Line 23 of the next 3 images.

AGRICULTURAL CENSUS—ENUMERATION DISTRICT, No. 1 in the Township OF

East Flamboro in the **COUNTY OF** Wentworth

Name of occupier.	Concession or Range.	Lot or part of Lot.	Held by each person or family.	Under Cultivation.	Under Crops in 1851.	Under Pasture 1851.	Gardens or Orchards.	Under Wood or Wild.	Wheat Acres.	Wheat Produce Bsh.	Barley Acres.	Barley Produce Bsh.	Rye Acres.	Rye Produce Bsh.
1	2	3	4	5	6	7	8	9	10	11	12	13	14	15
John Eaton	8	8	62	40	15	23	2	22	10	190	0	0	0	0
James McEwen	8	8	12	12	11	1	0	0	10	150	0	0	0	0
John Dillon	8	7	160	60	39	30	1	40	14	200	0	0	0	0
John Whitfield	8	8	50	40	30½	19	½	10	7	95	0	0	0	0
Samuel Eaton	7,8	8,9	150	69	40	37	3	81	21	450	0	0	0	0
George Bradt	8	9	5	2½	1½	1	0	2½	1	20	0	0	0	0
John C. [illegible]	4	7	100	40	37	11	3	60	8	120	8	100	0	0
Johnson Skipper	5	8	100	40	26	13	1	60	12	200	2	40	0	0
Jeffry Breedon	6	7,8	200	13	7	6	0	187	4	150	0	0	0	0
Ann Attridge Sen	6	8	100	35	26½	7½	1	65	6½	100	0	0	0	0
Andrew Attridge	6	9	50	30	23½	7	½	20	6½	124	0	2	0	2
Saml Gallagh	6	8	100	40	30	19½	½	60	8	150	0	0	0	0
William Attridge	6	9	50	20	6	14	0	30	3	70	0	0	0	0
Joseph [illegible]	7	9	50	22	3	19	0	28	0	0	0	0	0	0
William Shankle	7	8	22	7	1	6	0	15	0	0	0	0	0	0
Michael Mills	7	7	50	14	8½	5	½	36	4	180	0	0	0	0
James Kevine	7	8	25	6	½	5½	0	19	0	0	0	0	0	0
Nelson Madden	7	8	78	12	7	5	0	36	3	45	0	0	0	0
Henry Mockler	7	7	30	8	5½	3½	0	12	4	80	0	0	0	0
Alex McDougall	7	7	100	65	29	36	0	35	14	300	0	0	0	0
Andrew Patton	8	3,6,7	251	40	17	21	2	270	6	120	0	0	0	0
Jno Lamton	8	2	100	60	30	29½	½	40	18	180	0	0	0	0
John Galloway	9	2	100	30	17½	12½	0	70	10	200	1	20	0	0
Richard [illegible]	8	1	100	30	16½	13½	0	70	6	60	0	0	0	0

	Peas		Oats		B. Wheat		Indian Corn		Potatoes		Turnips		Clover, Timothy or other grass seed—Bsh.	Carrots—Bsh.	Mangle Wurzel
	A	Bsh	A	Bsh	A	Bsh	A	Bsh	A	Bsh	A	Bsh			
	16	17	18	19	20	21	22	23	24	25	26	27	28	29	30
1	0	0	0	0	0	0	½	40	½	40	0	0	0	0	0
2	0	0	0	0	0	0	0	0	1	100	1	0	0	0	0
3	5	100	4	100	3	80	½	20	½	50	0	0	0	0	0
4	2½	20	3	100	1	18	½	50	½	60	0	0	0	0	0
5	0	0	3	150	7	40	4	80	½	40	½	50	0	0	0
6	3	0	0	0	0	0	0	0	0	20	0	0	0	0	0
7	0	0	8	200	0	0	0	0	½	50	0	0	0	0	0
8	4½	60	6	150	0	0	0	0	½	50	0	0	0	0	0
9	0	0	½	20	0	0	0	0	¾	30	0	0	0	0	0
10	0	0	7	300	0	0	½	30	2	160	0	0	0	0	0
11	0	0	0	0	0	0	½	20	1	80	0	0	0	0	0
12	1	14	5	100	0	0	0	0	1	40	1	60	0	0	0
13	0	0	0	0	0	0	0	0	1	50	0	0	0	0	0
14	0	0	0	0	2½	60	2	20	½	18	0	0	0	0	0
15	0	0	0	0	0	0	0	0	½	30	0	0	0	0	0
16	0	0	0	0	0	0	0	0	½	40	0	0	0	0	0
17	0	0	0	0	0	0	0	0	½	10	0	0	0	0	0
18	0	0	0	0	0	0	0	0	¼	25	0	0	0	0	0
19	0	0	0	0	0	0	0	0	0	0	0	0	0	0	0
20	1	40	0	0	1	50	0	0	1	40	0	0	0	0	0
21	0	0	2	65	0	0	3	40	2½	800	0	0	0	0	0
22	0	0	0	0	1	15	0	0	½	25	1	150	0	0	0
23	0	0	0	0	0	0	0	0	1	130	½	100	0	0	0

	Beans Bsh.	Hops Lbs.	Hay. Bundles or Tons	Flax or Hemp Lbs.	Tobacco Lbs.	Wool Lbs.				Maple Sugar. Lbs.	Cider Galls.	Fulled Cloth Yards.	Linen—Yds.	Flannel—Yds.
	31	32	33	34	35	36	37	38	39	40	41	42	43	44
1	0	0	6	0	0	36				0	0	0	0	0
2	0	0	0	0	0	10				0	0	0	0	60
3	0	0	18	0	0	50				0	18	30	0	45
4	0	0	11	0	0	35				160	0	20	0	25
5	0	0	15	0	0	90				10	0	20	0	36
6	0	0	0	0	0	10				0	0	0	0	0
7	0	0	4	0	0	0				0	0	0	0	0
8	0	0	1	0	0	12				0	0	0	0	0
9	0	0	3	0	0	0				0	0	0	0	0
10	0	0	10	0	0	30				0	0	15	0	10
11	0	0	20	0	0	11				0	0	0	0	20
12	0	0	7	0	0	60				0	0	30	0	47
13	0	0	4	0	0	0				0	0	0	0	0
14	0	0	0	0	0	0				0	0	0	0	0
15	0	0	0	0	0	16				0	0	0	0	36
16	0	0	6	0	0	18				50	0	0	0	0
17	0	0	0	0	0	0				0	0	0	0	0
18	0	0	5	0	0	18				10	0	10	0	8
19	0	0	2	0	0	0				0	0	0	0	30
20	0	0	20	0	0	40				100	0	19	0	0
21	0	0	5	0	0	0				0	0	0	0	0
22	0	0	15	0	0	47				0	0	0	0	60
23	0	0	7	0	0	0				0	0	0	0	0
24	0	0	10	0	0	17				[illegible]	[illegible]	[illegible]	[illegible]	[illegible]

"From Pathway to Skyway" by Claire Emery and Barbara Ford. Published by Confederation Centennia Commitee of Burlington. Burlington Ontario 1967

Chapter 13: Kilbride

In 1853 land on the south side of No. 5 Sideroad west of Cedar Springs Road had been deeded by John Prudham to the trustees. Mr. Prudham's homestead south of Kilbride had been a stopping place for itinerant ministers. Mr. Prudham and Mathias Canon both of Nelson, along with Jonas Vollick, Andrew Davidson and Richard Vollick were the original trustees of the small church of the Methodist New Connexion called Bethel Chapel. The union of exiting Methodist bodies caused Bethel to close about 1874 but a committee of trustees was appointed to care for the grounds and cemetery.

1861 Census East Flamborough D-4 C-1086 p. 58 Line 43

43	Rich.d Vollick	L.	C W	N C M	52
44	Eliz.h Do		Do	Do	45
45	Lovina Vollick		Do	Do	20
46	Eliza Do		Do	Do	18
47	Daniel Do		Do	Do	16
48	John Do		Do	Do	14
49	Matilda Do		Do	Do	12
50	Melissa Do		Do	Do	10

1871 census Hay Township Huron Co. C 6 L. 16 he is a tenant on land with Haggai Shuart and Clarissa Robins and family.

Sometime between the 1871 census and the 1881 census, Elizabeth (Burkholder) Vollick died. I have not found a death record or burial site for her.

1881 census Huron Co. Hay Tp #2, p 24 Reel C13272

1891 census Hay Tp Huron South

Richard died in Hay Township on 17 July 1891

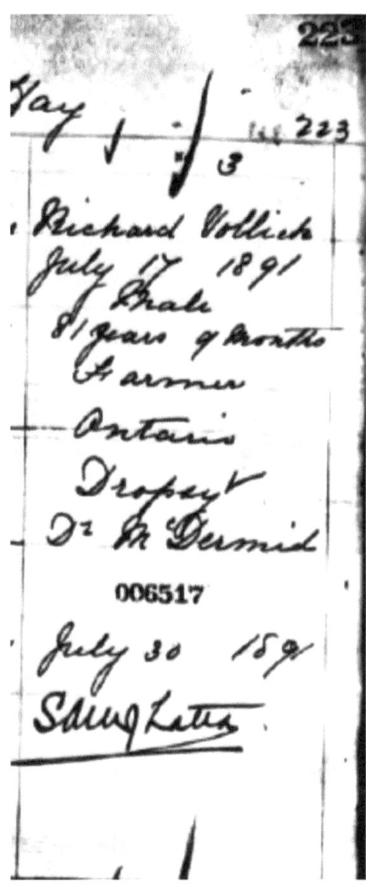

Richard Vollick and Elizabeth Burkholder were married before 1832 in Ontario. They had the following children:

i. Isaac Vollick was born on 16 Jan 1831 in Upper Canada. He married Lydia Jamieson before 1858. He died on 25 Mar 1904 in Conc 5, Flos Township, Simcoe Co. Ontario.

ii. Sarah Vollick was born on 26 Feb 1834. She died on 28 Oct 1856 in Kilbride, Nelson Township Halton Co. Ontario.

iii. Henry Vollick was born on 08 Oct 1835 in Nelson Township, Halton Co. Upper Canada. He married Rebecca Morden on 11 Nov 1868 in Nelson Township Halton Co. Ontario. He died on 13 Nov 1916 in Nelson Township Halton Co. Ontario.

iv. David Vollick was born on 06 Oct 1839 in Ontario. He married Emeline Place on 07 Mar 1860 in East Flamborough Township Halton Co. Ontario. He died on 03 Nov 1920 in Toledo, Lucas Co. Ohio.

v. Ann Matilda (Matilda) Vollick was born between 1841-1849 in Halton Co. Ontario. She married George Parker on 22 Nov 1883 in Belgrave Village, Morris Tp, Huron County. She died on 13 Aug 1889 in Hay Tp, Huron Co. Ontario.

vi. Levina Vollick was born about 1841 in Ontario. She married Henry May in 1861. She died after 1880 possibly in Grand Rapids Michigan.

vii. Elizabeth (Eliza) Vollick was born about 1844 in Ontario. She married William Grandy on 04 May 1864 in Hay Township, Huron Co. Ontario. She died on 26 Mar 1882 in Clyde, St. Clair Co., Michigan.

viii. Daniel Vollick was born on 21 Jul 1845 in Hay Tp Huron Co. Ontario. He died after 1881.

ix. John (Jonas) Vollick was born in Feb 1847 in East Flamboro Tp Ontario. He married Susannah Mariah Shuart on 01 Jul 1873 in Exeter, Hay Tp Huron Co. Ontario. He died on 23 May 1918 in Bayfield, Huron Co. Ontario.

x. Melissa Vollick was born on 25 Oct 1851 in Ontario. She married George McDonald on 06 Dec 1870 in Seaforth, Huron Co. Ontario. She died on 29 Apr 1930 in Detroit, Wayne, Michigan.

Margaret Vollick & David Burkholder

1842 census Nelson Township Gore District shows David Burkholder, Labourer, 7 natives of Canada. 1 male under 5 years of age, 2 females under 5 years of age, 2 males ages 5 to 14 years, 1 married person age 30 to 60; 1 married person age 14 to 45.

1851 Census District: Norfolk County District Number: 25 Sub-District: Middleton Sub-District Number: 235 Page: 35 Line: 35 Roll: C_11741

Margaret (Vollick) Burkholder died after this 1851 census but before 12 January 1852

1865: East Flamborough Township Directory: David Burkholder is on Conc 8 Lot 5.

1881 Census Norfolk North, Sub-District Number: B, Subdistrict: Townsend, Division: 2

David Burkholder and Margaret Vollick were married in 1831. They had the following children:

i. Jacob Wesley Burkholder was born about 1833.

ii. George Burkholder was born about 1835.

iii. Eliza Jane Burkholder was born about 1837 in Milton, Ontario. She married John Charles King on 03 Jul 1861 in East Flamborough Township. She died on 15 April 1916 in South Norwich, Oxford Co. Ontario.

iv. Mary Ann Burkholder was born on 05 Jan 1841 in Nelson Township Halton Co. Ontario. She married Isaac Bradt in 1864 in Waterdown Ontario. She died on 05 Oct 1910 in Allenville, South Norwich, Oxford Co. Ontario.

v. Cornelius Harvey (aka Henry) Burkholder was born in 1844 in East Flamborough Tp, Wentworth Co. Ontario. He married Almeda Burch on 13 Dec 1900 in Burford, Brant Co. Ontario. He died on 27 May 1923 in Burford, Brant Co. Ontario.

vi. David Burkholder was born in 1845.

vii. Hannah Burkholder was born on 23 Dec 1847 in Ontario. She died on 20 Oct 1933 in Brantford, Brant Co. Ontario.

viii. Maria Elizabeth Burkholder was born on 14 Jun 1848 in West Flamboro, Wentworth Co. Ontario. She died on 23 Feb 1927 in Wentworth Co. Ontario.

ix. John Burkholder was born about 1849.

x. Phoebe Catherine Burkholder was born about 1851 in Ontario. She died on 19 July 1914 in South Norwich, Oxford, Ontario.

The Larroway Family

While I have done extensive research on the Larroway family and their spouses, it is beyond the scope of this book to write up their complete ancestry and story. It is my hope that the following details of the family ancestry will be helpful to descendants.

Generation 1
Simeon Le Roy-dit-Audy b: 1637 in Coutances, France, d: Aft. 1706 in Ulster Co. New York married Claude Des Chalets b: About 1651 in France, m: 03 Sep 1668 in Quebec, d: Aft. 1706 in Ulster Co. New York USA

The origin of the LeRoy family of Dutchess County, New York is discussed in *"Dictionaire Genealogique Des Familles Canadiennes"*. A five page article called *"The Life And Family Of Simeon Leroy"* was published about Simeon in the New York Genealogical & Biographical Record, volume 64, pages 41-45. Note that there are errors in both these articles so descendants would be wise to use them only for clues.

Simeon LeRoy was born in Creances which is a village about twelve miles northwest Of Coutances, Manche, Normandy. Simeon was married to Claude (aka Blandina) Deschalets in 1668 in the parish of Notre Dame in Quebec Canada by h. De bernieres. Their witnesses were Pierre Chamare, Michel Riffaut, and Francois Charlet. The parish register reads:

"the third day of the month of September, 1668, after betrothal and the publication of one bann of marriage, between Simeon LeRoy, a son of Richard LeRoy and Gilette Jacquet, his father and mother, of the parish of Notre Dame De fontenay le Comte, Bishopric Of Maitzais (Maillezais), of the second part;Monseigneur the bishop having granted them a dispensation of two banns, and there being discovered no legal impediment, I, the undersigned, Cure of this parish, have married them and have given them the nuptial benediction, according to the form prescribed by the Holy Church in the presence of the Known witnesses, Pierre Chamare, Michel Riffaut, Francois Charlet. (signed) H. De bernieres."

Simeon settled first in the fief or seigneurie of St.-Joseph or L'espinay, Charlesbourg, near the Charles River which belonged to the Hebert-Couillard de L'espinay family in Quebec, Canada in October 1668 (greffe:Notary Jean leconte, Quebec).

His neighbors were his brother-in-law, Jean Giron and Andre Barbaut. He was a resident of St. Joseph's from 1668 to 1679. On December 13, 1676 Simeon bought a lot with an untenantable house in Quebec (greffe: Notary Pierre Duquet, Quebec). The purchase price was discharged in part October 25, 1678 out of an advance of 100 livres paid to him on account of carpentry work contracted by him to be done for the sisters of the congregation of montreal. It is not known what building he was to erect for the sisters. He was in Montreal in July 1679 and bought considerable land there that fronted on the St. Lawrence River in Cote St.-Francois (greffe: Notary Maugue, Montreal). The deed dated July 2, 1679 calls him a resident of Quebec but as of July 30, 1679 becoming a resident of Montreal.

Simeon also bought land in Montreal on April 10, 1680, December 9, 1680 and January 4, 1681. He entered into building contracts on September 7, 1680 and December 22, 1680. On January 6, 1681 he surveyed some land to estimate the amount of timber on it. On May 15, 1681 Simeon contracted with Antoine Guibord and Francois Huart to work for him as sawyers. The census of 1681 shows Simeon LeRoy and his wife Claude and their 8 children as residents of Montreal. Simeon's last appearance in the records of Montreal was at the time of the burial of his daughter Marie on May 21, 1681. The next appearance of Simeon on any public record found so far is in Albany, New York when on November 28, 1682 he apprenticed his son Augustin, age 11 to Adam Winne to learn ropemaking for 6 consecutive years.

Sometime between May 1681 and November 1682 Simeon took or sent his second son Jean to St. Joseph, Charlesbourg to live with his godfather, Jean Giron. He then took his wife and their young children to Albany, New York. Around 1689 he moved to Kingston, Ulster County, New York. In 1689 he rented a house that beonged to Jochem Hendrickse (greffe: notary Maugue, Montreal). Before 1701 he bought a house and lot from Henry Beekman (Albany notarial papers in the county Clerk's office, volume 2, page 420). Simeon fell on hard times in his old age. The Minutes Of The Trustees of Kingston, March 1, 1708 show that on that date Simeon was given a pair of shoes and a load of wood. The trustees also paid for the burial of his wife. It is thought that Simeon died soon after his last mention in the Ulster County tax list of 1710.

Simeon's name can be found in the Kingston records for the years 1686 or 1687, 1689, 1691, 1693, 1695, 1697, 1701, 1707, 1708, and 1710.

Claude "Blandina" was one of three orphaned sisters who were sent to Canada as a "Filles Du Roi"(King's Daughters). The Filles Du Rois were impoverished or oprhan women sent to Canada at royal expense to find husbands and populate the country. She was probably recently arrived in New France (now Quebec) at the time of her marriage because the bishop dispensed with two of the usual three required banns for rer marriage to Simeon LeRoy.

The Filles du Roi, or King's Daughters, consisted of 770 women who arrived in the colony of New France (Canada) between 1663 and 1673 under the financial sponsorship of King Louis XIV of France. Most were single French women and many were orphans. The King paid their transportation to Canada and settlement in the colony. Some were given a royal gift of a dowry of 50 livres for their marriage to one of the many unmarried male colonists in Canada.

In 1669 Claude and her sister Madeleine Deschalets Giron were summoned before the Sovereign Council of New France because of their scandalous talk about the conduct of Francoise Leclerc, the wife of Michel Riffaut on the ship coming to New France. Francoise Leclerc was also a Filles Du Roi. Claude and Madeleine were accused of maliciously and falsely calling Francoise Leclerc a prostitute. They were required to apologize and pay a small fine. Michel Riffaut had been a witness at the marriage of Simeon and Claude Deschalets LeRoy the preceding year.

Generation 2
Leonard-Tremi (aka Jonas) Le Roy b: 15 Sep 1674 in St. Joseph, Charlesbourg, Quebec, d: Aft. 1750 in Schoharie Co. New York married Maria Uziele b: About 1686 in Staten Island, New York, m: 28 Sep 1703 in Kingston, Ulster Co. New York, d: Before 1750 in Schoharie New York

Leonard-Tremi LeRoy was baptized on 18 Sep 1674 in Quebec. Leonard-Reni (aka Treny aka Tremi) LeRoy's name was corrupted in the Dutch records to the phonetically similiar "Jonar Larua". It is under this name that he appears in most New York records. He settled at Schoharie, New York and produced the Laraway family, many of whom were Loyalists who fled to Upper Canada (Ontario) during the American Revolution. Some of his descendants chose to return to the LeRoy spelling. As Jonas Laraway he died sometime after 1750.

Generation 3
Petrus Le Roy b: 03 Sep 1704 in Kingston, New York, d: Schoharie New York married Marytie Van Alstyne b: 31 Oct 1708 in Kinderhook, New York, m: 16 Oct 1730 in New York

Generation 4
Jonas Larroway b: About 1731 in Schoharie New York, d: Aft. 1801 in Ontario married Elizabeth Muller b: 30 Mar 1735 in Germantown, New York, m: 16 Feb 1754 in Schoharie, Schoharie, New York

Generation 5
Eve Larroway b: 14 Mar 1776 in Berne, Albany Co. New York married Cornelius Vollick b: 16 Aug 1761 in Albany New York, m: 24 Mar 1795 in Niagara, Ontario, d: Aft. 1818 in Ontario

The Burkholder Family

Generation 1

Jacob Burkholder b: Apr 1747 in Ementhal Switzerland, d: 02 Mar 1817 in Hamilton,
Barton Township Wentworth Co. Ontario married Sophia De Roche b: 21 May 1748
in France, m: Lancaster Co. Pennsylvania, d: 09 Apr 1839 in Hamilton, Barton
Township Wentworth Co. Ontario

Jacob and Sophia were the first settlers in Hamilton on land called the Burkholder
Settlement. A monument to them was erected in 1949.

Jacob Burkholder and his two brothers, John and Christian sailed for America in
1765 on the ship *Myrtilla*. They landed at Philadelphia, 21 September 1765. John
and Jacob Burkholder settled in Lampeter Township, Lancaster Co., Pennsylvania,
while Christian Burkholder settled near Newbury in Franklin Co., Pennsylvania.

Several French Huguenot refugees were among the *Myrtilla's* 81 passengers,
including Abraham and Sophia De Roche. Sophia was a French girl, supposedly of
Huguenot descent. Jacob married Sophia De Roche in 1765 in Lancaster Co.,

Pennsylvania. Their signatures may be seen in Pennsylvania, where they took the oath of allegiance to the British Crown in 1765.

Following the American Revolution Jacob Burkholder wished to remain under British rule. It is important to note however that they were not Loyalists. After his eldest sons made an exploratory trip to the head of Lake Ontario, Jacob, Sophia and family left Pennsylvania for Upper Canada (now the province of Ontario). With their son Christian as their guide, they came by Conestoga wagon drawn by oxen, crossing at Buffalo and arriving at Niagara in present day Ontario in July 1794. They obtained 800 acres on the Hamilton Mountain and were the first family to settle east of the Caledonia highway.

They settled on the escarpment in the eastern part of Barton Township, Wentworth County on lot 9 concession 6. Eventually the various members of the family received crown patents to some 600 acres on lots 8-11 Concession 6 and lots 9-10 Concession 5.

In August 1794 Jacob and his two sons Christian and Jacob Jr. submitted petitions for land in what was then called the 8th Township (now Barton Township). Unfortunately an error was made in the spelling of their names and their petitions were granted under the surname of Borghonder. 21 years later the men filed another set of petitions and affidavits explaining the mistake and requesting that their deeds be granted as they had lived on the land and made improvements since August 1794. Friends and neighbours signed affidavits stating that this was all true and correct.

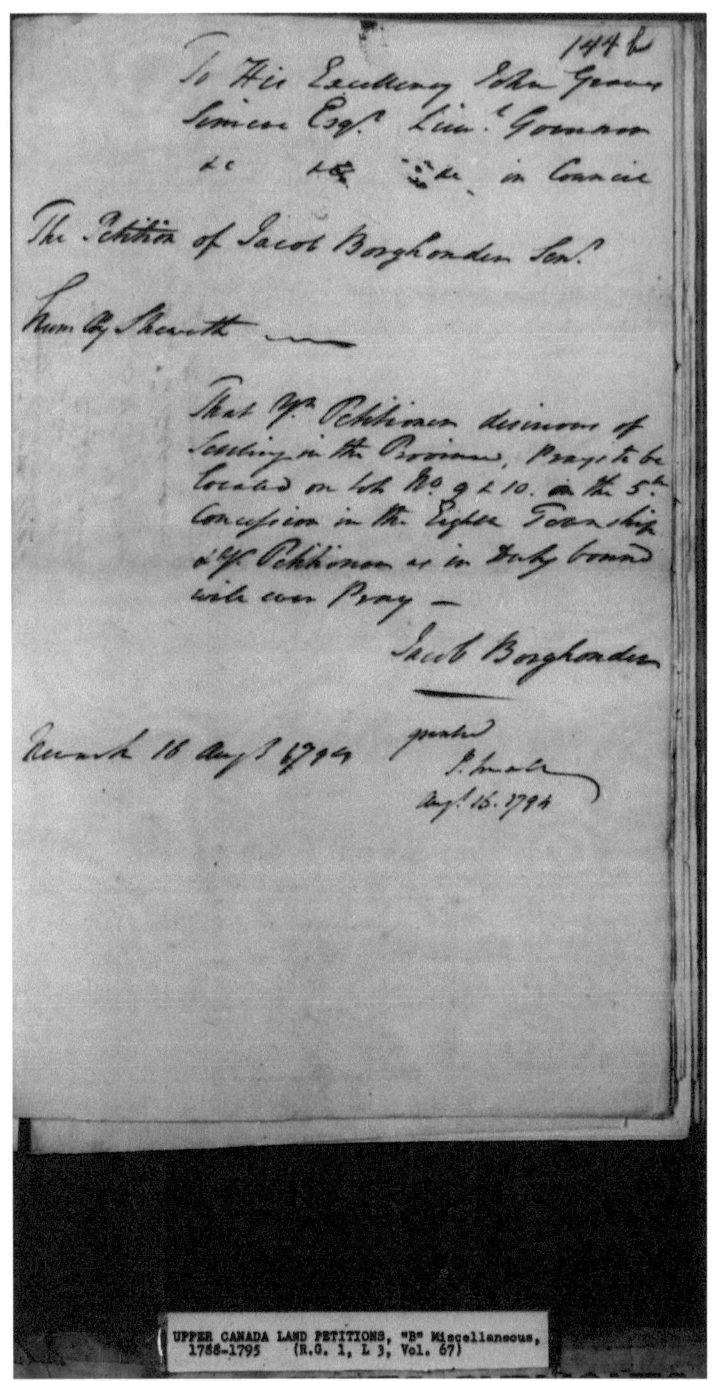

1794 Petition of Jacob Borghonder [sic] Sr.

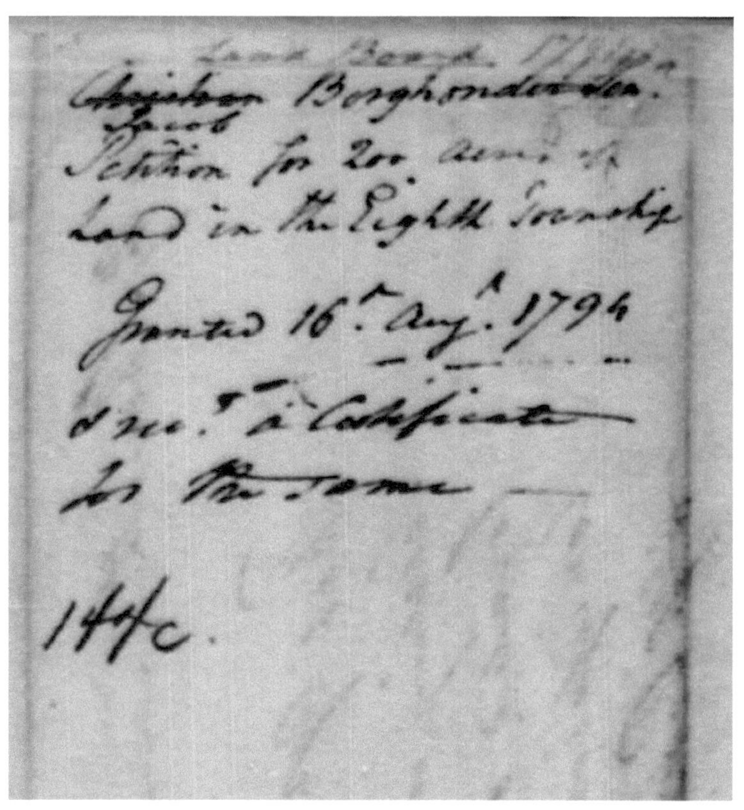

1794 Petition of Jacob Borghonder [sic] Sr.

To His Excellency Francis Gore Esquire
Lt. Governor of the Province of Upper Canada
&c &c &c

May it please Your Excellency!

In Obedience to your Excellencys order of reference to us, to report upon a certificate relative to Jacob Burkholder Senior and his Sons Christian Burkholder and Jacob Burkholder — we are to state for your Excellencys Information, that the undermentioned Lots are located and described in the Township of Barton, under the authority of three Land Board certificates —

		acres
To Jacob Borghonder Senior Lots No. 9 & 10 in the 5th Con.:		200
Christian Borghonder — Lots No. 8 & 9 in the 6 Con:		200
Jacob Borghonder Junr Lots No. 10 & 11 in the 6th Con:		200

All which is humbly submitted
to Your Excellencys Wisdom
Chewett & Ridout
acty Survey:r Genl

Survey:r Gen:l Office
York 7 Decemr 1807

(with the Certificates

1807 letter explaining lots granted to Borghonders

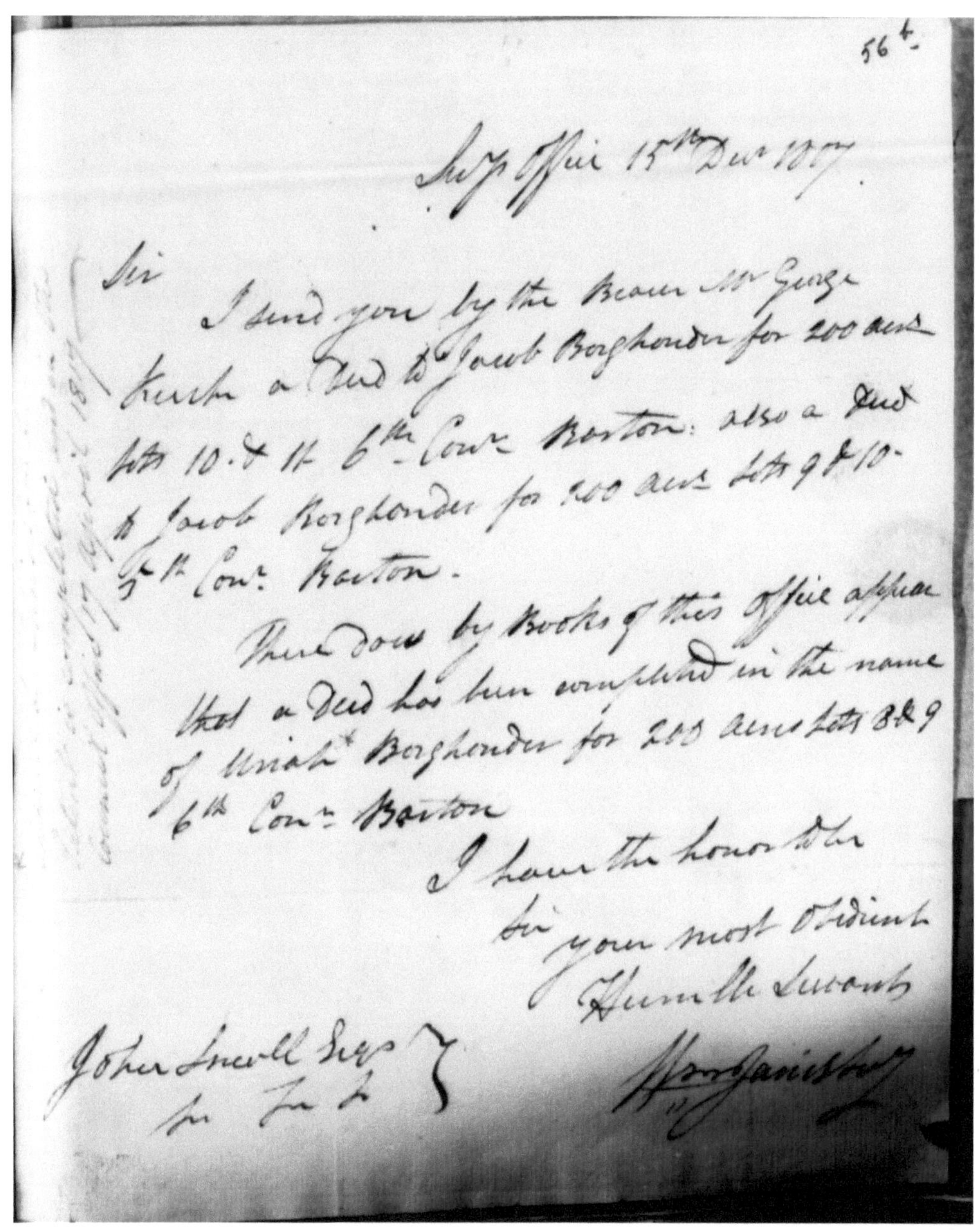

Surv[eyo]rs Office 15th Dec[embe]r 1807.

Sir

I send you by the Bearer Mr George
Hursh a Deed to Jacob Borghonder for 200 acres
Lotts 10 & 11 6th Conc[essio]n Barton: also a Deed
to Jacob Borghonder for 200 acres Lotts 9 & 10
5th Conc[essio]n Barton.

There does by Books of this Office appear
that a Deed has been completed in the name
of Uriah Borghonder for 200 acres Lotts 8 & 9
6th Conc[essio]n Barton

I have the honor to be
Sir your most Obedient
Humble Servant

[signature]

John Sewell Esq[uir]e
for ____

Dec. 1807 letter stating that deeds in the Surveyor's Office indicate the lands were granted in the name of Borghonder

April 1815 letter certifying that Jacob Burkholder came into Province July 1794 and submitted petition for land in August 1794

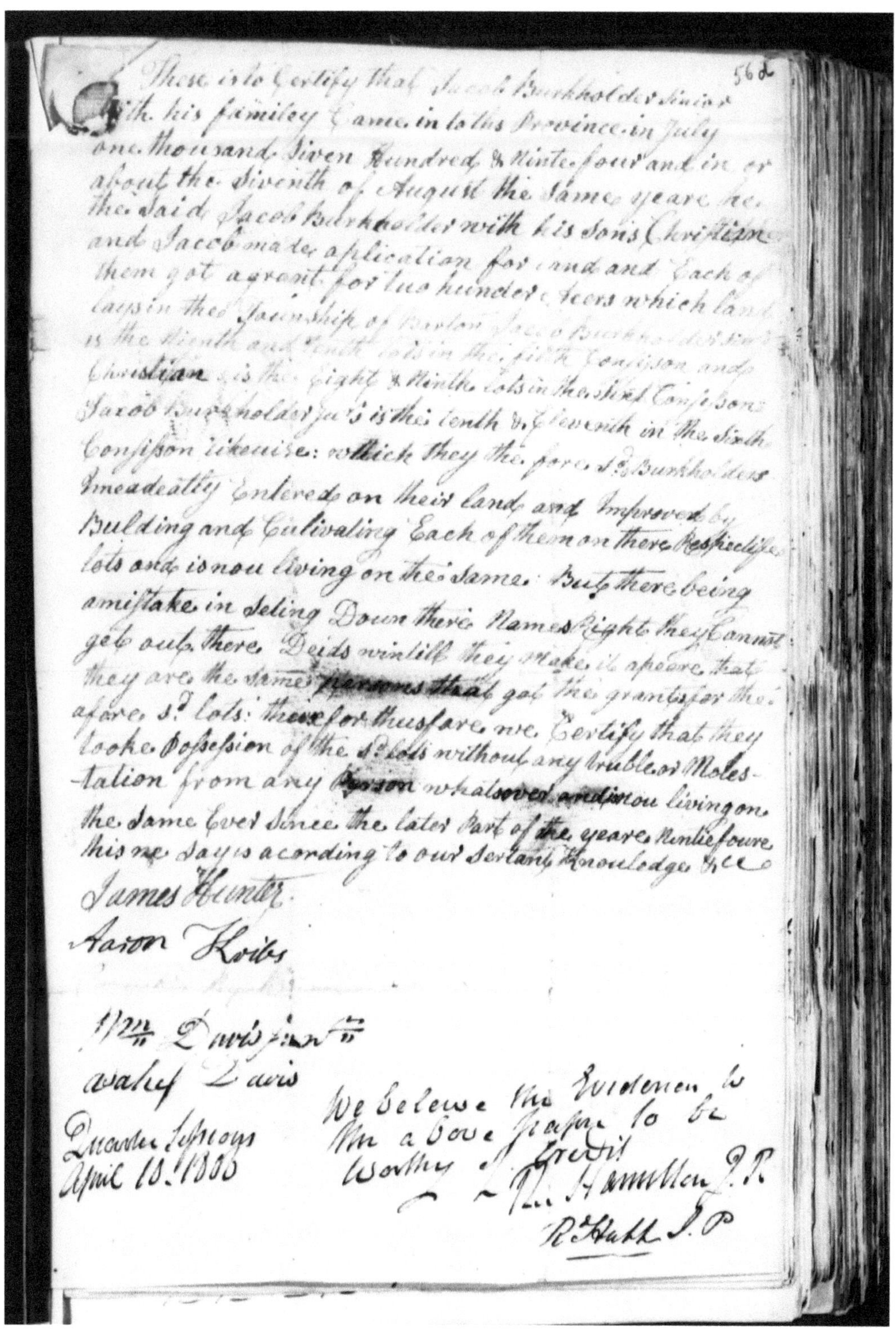

April 1806 affidavit supporting the Burkholders and explaining that because of the error in their names in the 1794 petitions, they have been unable to obtain their deeds on the lands in question

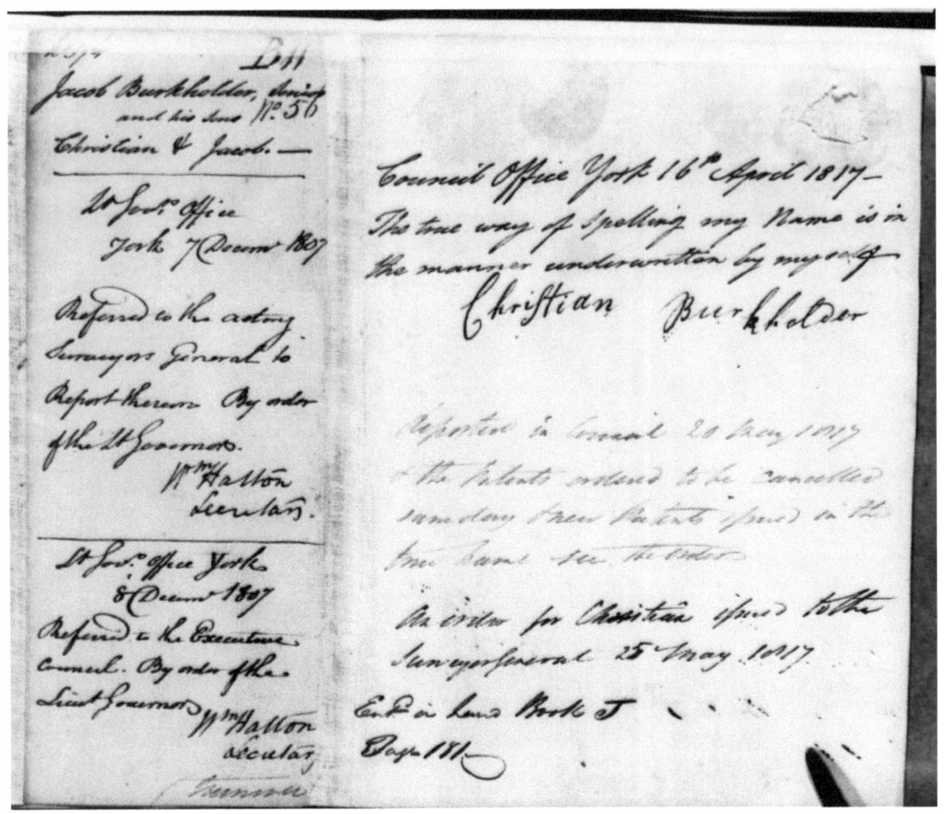

Envelope. Christian Burkholder signs his name and states that the correct spelling is as he has signed it (Burkholder). This envelope shows that in 1817 the old patents were cancelled and new patents issued in the correct names.

In 1808, Jacob was living on Lot 9, Conc. 5, Barton Tp., Wentworth County. His trade as a weaver helped support them in difficult times. During the first winter, Jacob turned to tailoring to supplement the family income and Peter Horning, who had been wearing buckskins up to this time, was reputedly his first customer.

Once settled, the Burkholders espoused the Methodist faith, probably influenced in part by the circuit riders who visited the district. The family made their home available for religious meetings. A family cemetery was established by 1800, the earliest interment being Burkholder's son Joseph, who died of a broken back after falling from a shed roof. The family gave its name to a small community, the Burkholder settlement, which developed at the intersection of what is now Mohawk Road and Sherman Avenue in Hamilton, Ontario. In 1839, a small log building was erected to serve as both church and school. It was replaced by the Mountain Chapel in 1850. This was renamed Burkholder Methodist Church in 1886 and after 1925, became known as Burkholder United Church.

Jacob Burkholder's date of death is not known. Different sources give 2 March 1812, 1813, and 1817 as possible dates.

BURKHOLDER, JACOB, pioneer, farmer, weaver, tailor; b. April 1747 in Switzerland; m. Sophia de Roche (Raich) in 1765 and they had four sons and two daughters; d. in Barton Township, Upper Canada, buried in the family cemetery (now part of Burkholder United Church Cemetery).

Generation 2
David Burkholder b: 10 Sep 1772 in Lancaster Co. Pennsylvania, d: 05 Oct 1843 in Barton Township Lincoln Co. Ontario married Elizabeth Gingerich b: About 1775 in Lancaster Co. Pennsylvania, m: About 1802

The following are chlldren of David and Elizabeth

Generation 3
Jacob Burkholder b: 1806 in Ontario, d: 1894 in Maladide Township Elgin Co. Ontario married Eliza Follick b: About 16 May 1817 in Ontario, m: 09 May 1848, d: 05 Jun 1892 in Malahide, Elgin Co. Ontario, m: 04 Mar 1844 in Nelson Township Halton Co. Ontario married Janine Vollick b: Aft. 1806 in Ontario, m: Before 1830, d: Before 1848 in Nelson Township Halton Co. Ontario

Generation 3
David Burkholder b: 1808 in Ontario, d: 09 Jun 1882 in Middleton Township, Norfolk Co. married Margaret Vollick b: 14 May 1815 in Upper Canada, m: 1831, d: Before 12 Jan 1852 in Middleton Township Norfolk Co. Ontario married next Laura Swain b: About 1809 in USA, d: Aft. 1881, m: 1863

Generation. 3
Sophia Burkholder b: About 1810 in Hamilton, Barton Township Wentworth Co. Ontario, d: Bet. 1881-1891 in Kilbride, Nelson Township Halton Co. Ontario married Isaac Vollick b: 24 Apr 1796 in Nelson Township Halton Co. Ontario, m: About 1827, d: 30 Apr 1864 in Nelson Township Halton Co. Ontario

Generation 3
Catharine Burkholder b: 23 Mar 1812 in Hamilton, Barton Township Wentworth Co. Ontario, d: 18 Jan 1864 in Hay Township, Huron Co. Ontario married Matthias Follick b: Bet. 1798-1800 in St. Catharines Ontario, m: Before Sep 1826, d: 11 Jan 1870 in Hay Township, Huron Co. Ontario

Generation 3
Elizabeth Burkholder b: About 1816 in Hamilton, Barton Township, Wentworth Co. Ontario, d: Bet. 1871-1881 in Hay Township, Huron Co., Ontario married Richard Vollick b: Oct 1809 in Upper Canada, m: Before 1832 in Ontario, d: 17 Jul 1891 in Hay Township, Huron Co. Ontario

Family Photographs

This section contains various family photogaphs. Some I own and others were kindly sent to me by other descendants. A huge thank you goes to individuals who so generously allowed photographs to be published in this book: Richard Smith, Don Hack, John Wright, Dodie Thurlow, Clara, Janelle Vassy, Linda Woods and many many others.

Each individual in the photos is named and their lineage back to Cornelis is summarized so that readers can see quickly how and where a photograph fits into our family. The way I have indicated the lineage is by use of the > symbol. For example a caption such as *"Cornelis> Richard> Isaac"* means Isaac was the son of Richard who was the son of Cornelis.

Henry Herbert Vollick 1883-1918
Cornelis>Richard>John>Henry

Henry Herbert
& wife Clara Harkness

Photos owned by Lorine McGinnis Schulze. Cololorizing by Mike Sharpe

Louisa Edwina Vollick born 1871

Cornelis>Matthias>William>Louisa

Belle Morgan & Edgar Miller Wedding
She was daughter of William Morgan & Louisa Edwina Vollick

Belle Morgan

William Morgan

Amanda Vollick 1829-1910
& Lovinia Vollick1834-1914

Cornelis>Jonas

The Van Norman – Hamilton – Crooker family.
Back row, left to right: Mary (Vollick) Church, George Church, Mary (Goodwin)
Van Norman, Frances (Rombough) Van Norman, William Crooker, C. Freeman
Van Norman, Mary Adelaide (Van Norman) "Auntie" Crooker, Myrtle Hamilton,
Richard Hamilton. Middle row: Ruby Church, John Van Norman, William Van
Norman, Amanda (Vollick) Van Norman, Ethel Hamilton, Delmer Vernon
Hamilton, Minerva Ann Hamilton holding Freeman Lorne Hamilton; Front row
(sitting on floor): Stanley Van Norman, Tracy Van Norman, Ernest Van Norman
Hamilton. — DONALD MACMILLAN

Lovinia Vollick 1834-1914
married James Davidson

Cornelis>Jonas

James Davidson

James & Lovinia Davidson with 9 of their 13 children

Livinia Vollick Davidson
1834-1915

Martha Davidson Briggs

Ruth Davidson Shaw
& daughter Bernice

Dorothy (Dolly) Davidson

Martha Davidson Briggs

Martha, Etta, Dolly
1935 Chicago

Nellie Davidson 1860-1917

Esther Vollick 1869-1920 married William Shuart

Esther Vollick & William Shuart
daughter Violet Shuart
grand-daughter Stella Morrell

Cornelis>Richard>Henry>Esther

Darwin Vollick 1885-1966
& Hazel Doonen Family

Cornelis>Isaac>William

Harriet Louise Folllick

Cornelis>Matthias>Enoch

Joseph Rife
& Elizabeth Follick
1826-1877

Cornelis>Matthias>Elizabeth

Elizabeth Bradt 1817-1866
& John Bridgeman

Cornelis>Mary>Elizabeth

Isaac Vollick & Lydia Jamieson

Cornelis>Richard>Isaac

Coffin Plate Isaac Vollick
owned by
Lorine McGinnis Schulze

Lydia Jamieson Vollick
with one of her sons

Lydia Jamieson Vollick

Children of Isaac Vollick & Lydia Jamieson

unknown daughter

Martha Vollick McGinnis
1874-1944

possibly
Serena Vollick Krull
1864-1944 -->

John Vollick 1871-1945

unknown son

Martha Vollick & Frederick McGinnis & children

Fred
1865-1921

Martha
1874-1944

I think this
is Martha
too -->

Mary & Lydia

McGinnis children ca 1924

Mabel, Mary, Lydia

Marriage
Certificate
James Vollick &
Sarah Quance
James > Isaac >
Richard> Cornelius

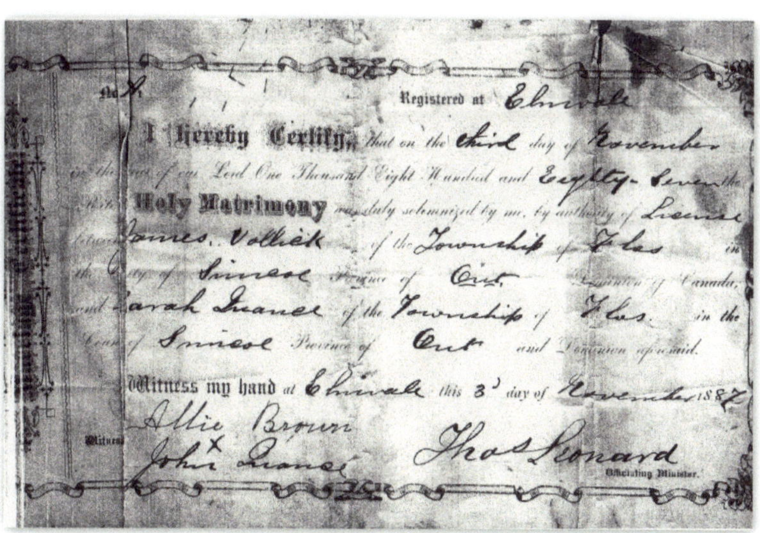

McGINNIS, John Archibald, Brigadier General (Retired), C.M., C.D. — Former Managing Director of the Toronto Historial Board and former Chairman of the Metro Toronto and Region Conservation Authority; former Commanding Officer, Queen's York Rangers (1st American Regiment) and later Commander, 15 Militia Group. Following that appointment, he was Senior Militia Advisor for Ontario. He died peacefully, surrounded by family members, on Sunday, February 14, 1999 at Sunnybrook Health Science Centre, following a short illness. He was 79. John McGinnis was born in Flos Township, Ontario, son of Frederick Joseph McGinnis and Martha Emily Vollick (van Valkenberg). He is survived by his wife Carol Gregory McGinnis, their children Martha and Gregory, and daughter-in-law Gayle. Predeceased by his first wife Margaret Scott McGinnis (in 1959) and survived by their daughter Diane Daniel of Toronto; sons Jon (Christine) and Ross of Brampton; grandsons Christopher and Sean Daniel (Kim Rowan) and Jeff McGinnis; great-grandchildren Ingrid Rowan and Galen Daniel-Rowan; and numerous nieces, nephews and their families. He served in the Royal Canadian Armoured Corps throughout W.W.II from 1939 in Canada, England and Northwest Europe, and subsequently in the Canadian Army Militia. He was Past President and Life Member of the Royal Canadian Armoured Corps Association; Past President, Royal Canadian Army Cadet League (Ontario); Life Member, Royal Canadian Military Institute; and Past President, Fort York Branch, Royal Canadian Legion. He was appointed Member of the Order of Canada in 1984 in recognition of his leadership in historical preservation. The family will receive friends at the HUMPHREY FUNERAL HOME - A.W. MILES CHAPEL, 1403 Bayview Avenue (South of Eglinton Ave. East), from 4:30-6:00 p.m. on Tuesday and Wednesday. Private interment. In lieu of flowers, donations to the Conservation Foundation of Greater Toronto, 5 Shoreham Drive, Toronto M3N 1S4 or to the Toronto Historical Board Trust Fund, 205 Yonge Street, Toronto M5B 1N2 would be appreciated.

Humphrey Funeral Home
A.W. Miles Chapel

Obit John McGinnis
son of Martha Vollick
& Frederick McGinnis

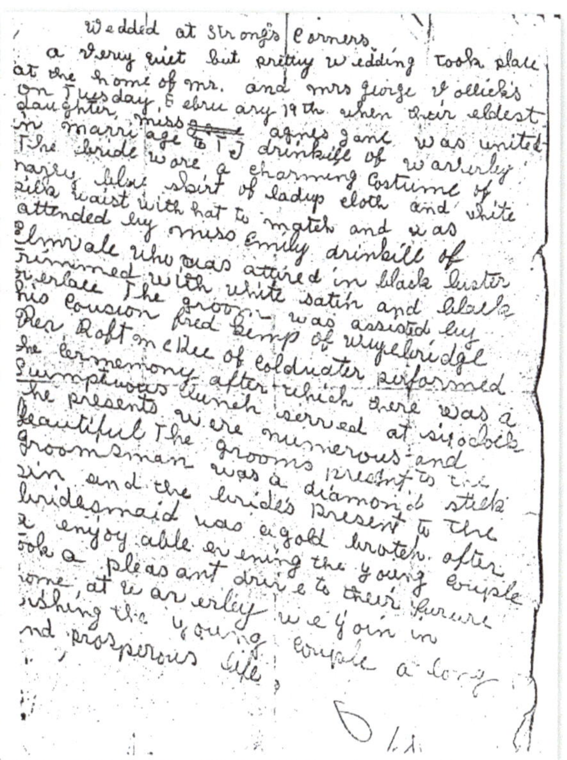

Writeup of wedding of
Agnes Vollick & Thomas Drinkell
Agnes > George > Isaac>
Richard> Cornelius

Albert Vollick 1869-1934
& Nellie Townes

Margaret Dobson Townes
& her daughters

Albert & Nellie Vollick & children

Joe
Grace
Laura
Lottie
Frank
Alvin
Fred
Gord
Isaac

Photo taken ca 1913

1866 Charles Vollick s/o
Isaac Vollick & Sophia
Burkholder
20th. Halton Regiment

Agnes Jane Vollick & Tom Drinkle
d/o George>Isaac>Richard>Cornelis

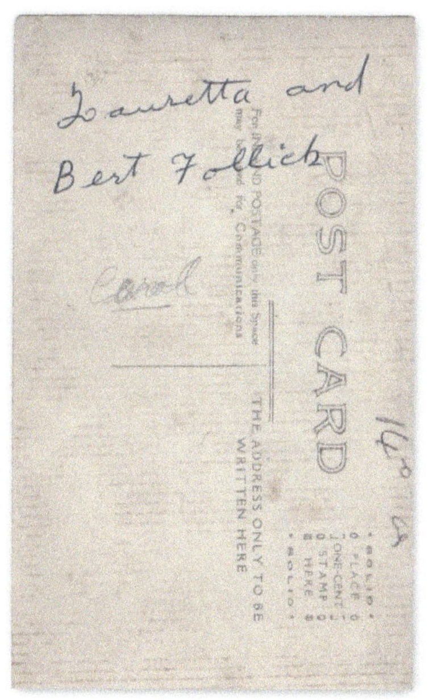

Lauretta Vollick & brother
Henry Herbert (Bert) Vollick 1883-1918
s/o John>Richard>Cornelis

Frances McGregor Gardner, Mary Madden, John, Jennie Turner, Fern Shelton, Wilbert, Orpha Markle

Frank Johnston & Cornelia Vollick
50th Wedding Anniversary
d/o William>Jonas>Cornelis

Sisters Pearl & Martha Vollick
d/o James>Isaac>Richard>Cornelis

Eileen Vollick 1908-1968
1st female pilot Canada
adopted d/o George>
Richard>Isaac>Cornelis

Peter James Vollick & Mary King
s/o James>Peter>Cornelis

96

Minnie Aukland wife of
William Clarkson Vollick s/o
William>Matthias>Cornelis

Ann Fenwick wife of
Enoch Follick
s/o Matthias> Cornelis

Fenwick Family
Grants Pass, Oregaon

Lovina Vollick 1871-1952
Morris>Jonas>Cornelis

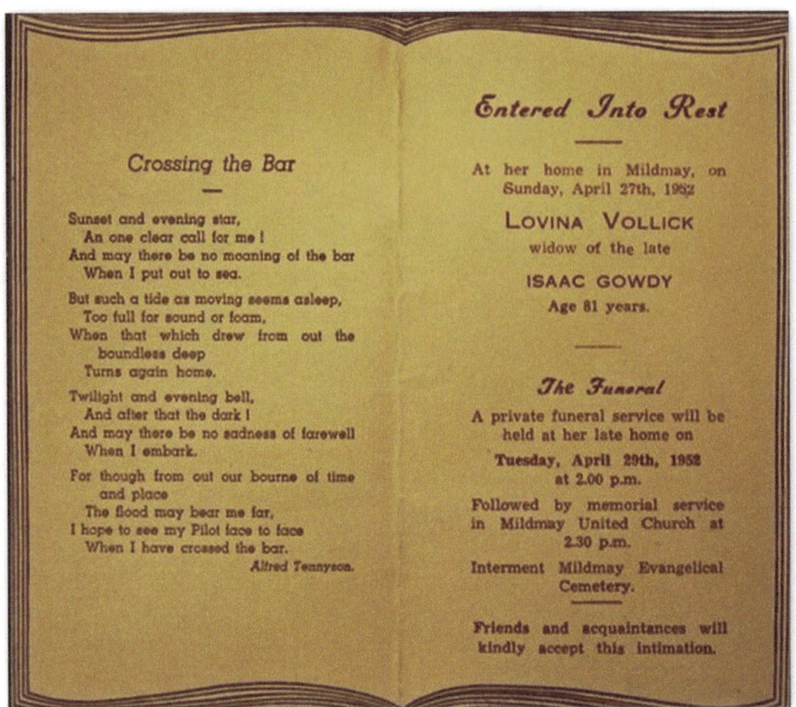

Isaac Gowdy
& his sons

Lovina's husband Isaac Gowdy
& his first wife Margaret Ney

back l -r Mary (Vollick) Church, George Church, Mary (Goodwin) Van Norman, Frances (Rombough) Van Norman, William Crocker, C. Freeman Van Norman, Mary Adelaide (Van Norman) "Auntie" Crooker, Myrtle Hamilton, Richard Hamilton

Middle row: Ruby Church, John Van Norman, William Van Norman, Amanda (Vollick) Van Norman, Ethel Hamilton, Delmer Vernon Hamilton, Minerva Ann (Van Norman) Hamilton holding Freeman Lorne Hamilton

Front row sitting on floor: Stanley Van Norman, Tracy Van Norman, Ernest Van Norman Hamilton. Photo Donald MacMillan

The Richard Hamilton family. Left to right seated: Richard, Ethel Winnefred, Freeman Lorne, Minerva Ann, Myrtle Theresa.

Standing at the back, from left, Delmer Vernon, Tracy Gilbert, Ernest Van Norman Hamilton. Photo Donald MacMillan.

Vollick Family Reunion, 1939. Courtesy Stephen Vollick

Half of the 1939 Vollick Family Reunion at Wasaga Beach, Ontario. Canada.

Front Row: x,x, Kenneth Robinson, Peter Robinson, x,x,x,x, Russell Cornelius Vollick, James Russell Eugene Vollick

2nd Row: x,x,x,x ,Stuart Vollick, rest unknown

3rd Row: x, Lila Vollick Robinson, x,x,x,x, William Mac Millan Vollick, Anna Mary Vollick, Walter James Vollick,rest unknown

4th Row: unknown

5th Row: x,x,x,x, Melinda Vollick,rest unknown

Newspaper Clippings

DIED

MOORE—At Barrie, March 26, John Moore, aged 72 years.

PEARSALL—At Oro Station, Wm. Milburn, son of Henry Pearsall, aged 23 months.

SMITH—In Allandale, on Friday, 25th March, 1904, John Benjamin Smith, in his 59th year.

SEXTON—At Vigo, March 25th, Jeremiah Sexton, aged 93 years.

VOLLICK—At Fergusonvale, March 25th, Isaac Vollick.

Barrie Examiner 31 Mar 1904

FERGUSONVALE

March 28—We are sorry to chronicle the death of Isaac Vollick which occurred at his home on Friday evening. The funeral took place, Monday, at Hillsdale. He leaves a widow and two unmarried sons.

Barrie Examiner 31 Mar 1904

—The cattle thieves, the Vollick brothers and French, were taken to the Central Prison on Tuesday.

Northern Advance 12 Dec. 1901

—Two brothers named Vollick pleaded guilty at Midland to stealing a heifer on Tuesday evening of last week from James Johnson on the 2nd Con., Flos. They were sent up for trial by Magistrates Ruby and Milligan in the absence of P. M. Storey. Chief Halloran brought them here to "the Castle" on Saturday.

Northern Advance 21 Nov. 1901

Died—Albert Vollick passed away at his home at Orr Lake on Saturday, January 27, 1934. The funeral was held at his late residence on Monday. Service was conducted by Rev. T. D. Jones and interment made in Elmvale cemetery.

Barrie Examiner 1 Feb. 1934

smart over the weekend.

Died—On Monday, January 29, 1934, Laura Drinkle, daughter of Mr. and Mrs. Thomas Drinkle, Waverley.

Barrie Examiner 1 Feb. 1934

LEAP YEAR TWINS

Notification has been received by The World of the second pair of twins to participate in the Leap Year Mug Award. The lucky parents are Mr. and Mrs. Herman Vollick of Foxmead, Ont. Two silver mugs have been forwarded.

As will have been seen from the letters which appeared in yesterday's World, these beautiful silver mugs, the work of Kent's Limited, are being very much appreciated by those who receive them. Coupons are still coming in, and it is likely that the mugs distributed will this year reach the 150 mark.

Toronto World 13 Mar 1912

Florence, the four-months-old daughter of Mr. and Mrs. Frank Vollick, Base line, died on Sunday, Nov. 16. The funeral service was held on Monday afternoon, Rev. E. E. Pugsley officiating, interment in Elmvale cemetery.

Barrie Examiner 20 Nov. 1924

erley, on Sunday.

Gwelda Lois Vollick, (twin) daughter of Mr. and Mrs. Gordon Vollick of Flos, died on Wednesday, Sept. 12, aged 3 months.

Barrie Examiner 20 Sept 1934

LOWVILLE.

May 15.

The funeral of the late Richard Vollick took place last Wednesday. There were a great many friends and relatives present. He was buried by the Waterdown Lodge, A.O.U.W., assisted by the Kilbride Lodge, the pall-bearers being Messrs. Clark, C. McMonies, C. Freeman and J. Tuck, of the former lodge, and Messrs. S. Nixon and G. Ellenton, of the latter. The deceased was highly respected by all who knew him, and the family have the sympathy of the entire community in their sad bereavement.

Canadian Champion 17 May 1900

DIED.

Ridd—At Huttonville, on Saturday, Nov. 11, 1916, John Ridd, in his 75th year.

Eaton—In Esquesing, on Monday, Nov. 6th, 1916, Sarah Eaton.

Vollick—At Nelson, on Monday, Nov. 13, 1916, Henry Vollick, in his 82nd year.

Canadian Champion 16 Nov 1916

Vollick—At Nelson, on Monday, Nov. 13, 1916, Henry Vollick, in his 82nd year.

Richard W. Vollick died at his home at Lowville on Monday, two days after a paralytic stroke. He had been a school teacher in Nelson for more than a quarter of a century and was in receipt of a pension for his long services. Latterly he had been a life insurance agent. He left a widow, two sons and five daughters.

Canadian Champion 10 May 1900

Finnemore-Vollick—In Hespeler, on Dec. 26th, at the residence of Orion Limpert, brother-in-law of the bride, assisted by Rev. W. S. Jamieson, Margaret J. Vollick, of Burlington, to Albert H. C. Finnemore, of Chicago.

Canadian Champion 7 Jan. 1904

Hounsome-Vollick—At the residence of the bride's aunt, fifth line, Nelson, on Jan. 14th, by the Rev. C. W. Vollick, uncle of the bride, Joseph Hounsome to Jenny Vollick, both of the township of Nelson.

Bradshaw-Bradley—At the home of

Canadian Champion 15 Jan. 1903

Inquest.—On the 19th ult., Roy Vollick, aged one month, illegitimate son of Mary Vollick, of Nelson, died under circumstances which neighbors considered suspicious and it was rumored that the child had been got rid of by an overdose of a narcotic medicine administered with that object. In consequence of the rumors County Attorney Matheson directed Coroner Freeman to hold an inquest, which was done last Friday. The evidence at the inquest proved that the child had died from inflammation of the lungs, not from poison, and the jury brought in a verdict to that effect and exonerating the mother from all blame.

Canadian Champion 3 April 1890

Died.

In Nelson on 22nd inst., the wife of Mr. Joseph Vollick of a son.

On Monday, 18th inst., the wife of John ——— of a daugh-

Canadian Champion 28 Mar 1867

SUDDEN DEATH.—We learn that a man by the name of Isaac Vallick, residing on the 5th line Nelson, died suddenly in a fit on Saturday last. Mr. Vallick, it appears has been slightly subject to fits for a length of time, and more especially if he was in trouble. This fit which proved fatal, was supposed to be induced in consequence of his having but the day previous been deprived of a daughter by that stern and relentless messenger—death. He leaves a family to mourn his demise.— *Milton Champion.*

Hamilton Evening Times 7 May 1864

MARRIED.

LESLIE—ROSS.—On December 4, at the residence of the bride's father, by the Rev. Mr. Cathcart, Presbyterian minister, Strabane, Herbert W. Leslie, of the township of Nelson, lately of Puslinch, to Catharine M. Ross, eldest daughter of David Ross, Puslinch, and formerly of Rosshire, Scotland.

MITCHELL—JOHNSTON.—On the 8th inst., at the residence of the bride's father, by Rev. R. Davey, Colin Mitchell, to Florence, second daughter of Captain Johnston, all of Esquesing township.

VOLLICK—SHARPE.—On Dec. 12th, at the residence of the bride's brother, T. Baker, 7 Devonport st., Hamilton, by Rev. A. C. Crews, Susan Sharpe, late of Melton, Mowbray, England, to Henry Vollick, of Nelson township.

Canadian Champion
20 Dec. 1888

Charged with non-support and for being drunk, William Vollick of Shunk road this morning was given a 90-day jail sentence suspended for six months. He was arraigned in justice court.

Michigan 12 Oct 1939

PROMISES TO SLAP NO MORE BICYCLE RIDERS

On a youth's word that he would slap no more bicycle riders, Judge Benjamin P. Jacobs today suspended a $5 fine assessed against Herman Couvier, 16, of 810 Augusta street, who was arrested Friday on complaint of Harold Vollick, 15, of Shunk road.

Vollick told Judge Jacobs that as he was riding his bicycle south on Ashmun street at Ann, a car driven by Couvier cut across in front of him and turned down Ann. Vollick said he shouted to Couvier that "he thought he was smart," and Couvier stopped the machine, got out, and slapped Vollick.

Pleading guilty to the assault charge, Couvier told Judge Jacobs that Vollick cursed in the presence of his mother, who was riding in the car.

Michigan 1939

FATAL ACCIDENT.—A fatal accident occurred on the 10th inst., at Mr. Hadden's mill, Nelson. A man by the name of Joseph Vollick was killed. It appears that he had been engaged at work on this mill for some time, acting in the capacity of fireman, and yesterday while in the act of throwing off the pump belt he was caught by it, and whirled around the main shaft at the rate of two hundred and forty times per minute. When they got the engine stopped, his body was a mutilated mass, the bones of his legs were broken to shivers. An inquest was held the same day on the body by Dr. Richardson, coroner, and a verdict of accidental death was given. No blame could be attached to either Mr. Hadden or Mr. Frazer, his foreman, as the mill is the same as any other mill, having a number of belts or straps, which always produce danger in dealing with them while in motion. He leaves a wife and five children to mourn his untimely end.

Canadian Champion
17 June 1869

MRS. DAVIDSON, WIDOW OF EARLY HOTELKEEPER, DEAD

AGED WOMAN, MOTHER OF LARGE FAMILY, HAS EIGHT DAUGHTERS AT DEATHBED

FUNERAL TOMORROW, 1.30 P. M.

Mrs. Lovina Davidson, long a respected resident of South Chicago, died at an early hour Saturday morning at the home of her daughter, Mrs. Jennie Mack, 224 E. 43rd street, Chicago, age 79 years.

Deceased was the wife of the late James Davidson, for many years engaged in the hotel business in South Chicago. Mr. Davidson died almost five years to the day from the date of his beloved wife's death — she on Jan. 18, 1914, he on Jan. 19, 1909.

Mrs. Lovina Davidson was a woman of grand character, beloved of all who had affiliated with her in life. Her's had been a life of constant devotion to those nearest her heart, and there were many, for she was the proud mother of nine daughters and two sons, all of whom survive her except one son, William Davidson, who died a few years ago. A notable feature, too, is the fact that eight of the nine daughters were present with this noble mother during her last hours.

Unswervingly she lived according to the precepts of the truest religion—adherence to the better elements of living—and this, coupled with her cheery disposition and constantly

Cook Co. Illinois
1914

John R. Alred, 21, of the Sault and Lillian Lozen, 21, of the Sault; Stanley R. White, 25, of Brimley and Jennie M. Vollick, 17, of the Sault, have filed application for marriage licenses at the office of Sam C. Taylor, county clerk.

28 Feb. 1939

from St. Marys a few years ago.

MAY 24, 1917

DR. FOLLICK'S MOTHER

(The Exeter Times)

Mrs. E. Follick celebrated her 80th birthday on Sunday last. Dr. L. L. Follick of St Marys motored over and visited his mother on that occasion and Mrs Gill of Grand Bend also spent the week-end with her sister. The occasion falling on "Mothers' Day" the grandchildren presented Mrs. Follick with a beautiful bouquet of flowers. In addition she was the recipient of other gifts and congratulations from distant friends. Although advancing in years, Mrs. Follick is still young in spirit and is hale and hearty. In extending our congratulations we wish for her continued years of health and happiness.

Thomas Henry Follick 1861-1928 son of Joseph son of Matthias son of Cornelis

Ann Fenwick, wife of Enoch Follick son of Matthias son of Cornelis. Her son Dr. L. L. is Leonard Laughlin Follick

Endnotes

[1] The Holland Society, *Baptism Record Albany Reformed Church, 1683-1804*, 16 Aug. 1761: His baptismal record shows his parents as Izak Valk and Marytje. Cornelia (this is obviously an error on the part of the transcriber, with the male name Cornelis being rendered as Cornelia due to similiarities in handwriting of the ending "a" and "s"). Sponsors: Coenraad Hoogtelling and Cornelia Hoogtelling

[2] Ontario Historical Society Papers & Records, *Early Records of St. Marks and St. Andrews Churches, Niagara Ontario*, (Vol. 3, 1901), Marriages 1795. Mar. 24. Cornelius Volick, br., and Eve Larraway, spinr.), daughter of Jonas Larroway and Elizabeth Muller.

[3] Courtesy of Brenda Young

[4] Upper Canada Land Book C 1st August, 1797 - 30th August, 1797

[5] Transcription from Salem Cemetery Kilbride

[6] Salem Cemetery Kilbride, Stone # 52: Isaac Vollick d. 30 Apr. 1864 aged 68 years and 6 days

[7] Salem Cemetery, Kilbride, BURIAL: has deeply cut stone: S.V.

[8] *Ontario Death Certificate*, Jonas VOLLICK, died Jan. 5, 1877, 79 years, 6 months, farmer born in Canada. Died of old age. Methodist.

[9] Buried Hillsgreen Cemetery. Inscription on tombstone reads *"In memory of Matthias Follick, who died 11th Januar 1870, aged 70 yrs, a native of St. Catharins [sic]."*

[10] Hillsgreen Cemetery, Catherine Follick, died Jan. 18, 1864 aged 52 years 4 mos and 5 days

[11] Vol. 1 page 22 8 Jan 1857

[12] Halton County Death Registrations, Nelson Township Albert Bradt died of dropsy. Son D. Bradt of Nelson was informant. Farmer, Baptist. 86 years old

[13] *Ontario Death Certificate*, Richard died at age 81 y. 9 mo. of Dropsy.

[14] Reel C13272, *1881 Census Hay Tp Huron Co.*, p 24.

[15] Ontario Historical Society Papers & Records, *Early Records of St. Marks and St. Andrews Churches, Niagara Ontario*, (Vol. 3, 1901), [This list of 41 names were baptized at the 12-Mile Creek on the same day.] 1815. May 14. Margaret Follick, of Cornelius and Eve.)

[16] 1851 Census, She died of Black Fever and Consumption at Middleton Township Norfolk Co. and is listed in the 1851 census under deaths.

[17] Ontario, Canada Deaths, 1869-1932 Elgin 1892, Malahide Township Eliza Burkholder, 75 years 20 days old, born Ontario, died of Dropsy from disease of the liver. had for 7 months. Slip for C W Marlatt. Baptist.

[18] Ontario Marriage Notices, Christian Guardian, 1836-1849. 10 Apr 1844 p 112. 4th March. Richard Lightheart and Eliza Follock both of Nelson. Rev Thomas Cosford

[19] Courtesy of Brenda Young